65p
13/-

Jim Barron of Nottingham Forest punches the ball safely over the bar to foil Arsenal's John Radford

THE ALL STARS FOOTBALL BOOK No. 11

edited by
JIM ARMFIELD

with special contributions by
JIM ARMFIELD
ALAN BIRCHENALL
GEOFF ELLIS
TONY GREEN
JOHN HOLLINS
GORDON JEFFERY
JULIAN JEFFERY
STAN LIVERSEDGE
LARRY LLOYD
BOBBY MONCUR
HENRY NEWTON
LESLIE PAGE
DON ROGERS
JOE ROYLE
DAVID SADLER

WORLD DISTRIBUTORS, PUBLISHERS, LONDON

CONTENTS

Picture Selections by GORDON JEFFERY

LIST OF ILLUSTRATIONS

about ourselves

BY sheer coincidence the underlying theme that seems to have interested several of our contributors this year is an awareness of the way this magic game of football is always changing. Jim Armfield himself decided to write about what he called 'The Changing Face of Soccer' and soon after along came Leslie Page's contribution —an article which he called 'The Changing Pattern of Football'!

David Sadler in his article mentions how 'the changing nature of the game itself often means that a player has to adapt himself to a newer role', whilst John Hollins, to give just one more example, considers the 1970 World Cup championship tournament in Mexico and its possible consequences by admitting that—

'Frankly, I don't know what will happen in the next few years. The England team, for some seasons the 4–4–2 supremos, were very quick to change to the more fluid 4–3–3 system for the first full international after the defeat in Mexico.'

The truth is, of course, that football has always been a changing game. Gordon Jeffery, who, in his article about some of the clubs who have been the 'tops' at different periods of the history of the Football League, goes further back into the past than any other contributor this time, could tell you how the style of play of Huddersfield, the great club of the twenties, differed vastly from that of Arsenal, the great club of the thirties—even though both were set on their paths to the top by the same great managerial genuis of football, Herbert Chapman.

It was, as a matter of fact, a change in the law of the game—the one affecting off-side—that was largely responsible for the change in style between the twenties and the thirties, and it can be argued that once the WM formation of the thirties had become generally used in British football there was a relatively long period of no change. Some would say it became a period of stagnation from which we in Britain were only jolted when the Hungarians came to Wembley in 1953 and soundly thrashed the English national team by six goals to three!

British clubs, almost without exception, had played until that time without much regard for the way in which the game had changed elsewhere in the world. Since then increasingly, and the way in which air travel has made it possible to quickly fulfil fixtures anywhere in the world has helped in this—as has also the televising of matches from other countries, we have accepted that football is a world game and so the incidence of changing patterns will be greater.

Echoes of the last World Cup and thoughts about the next one in 1974 crop up in several of our articles but it is worth remembering some words of Larry Lloyd—'But as for 1974 . . . we'll wait and see. I'M still busy concentrating on holding down my first-team place in the First Division with Liverpool. And THAT will do for me to be going on with.'

That is well said—it will be the battles for Cup and League at home that will most concern us for the next two years.

The Changing Face of SOCCER

by JIM ARMFIELD

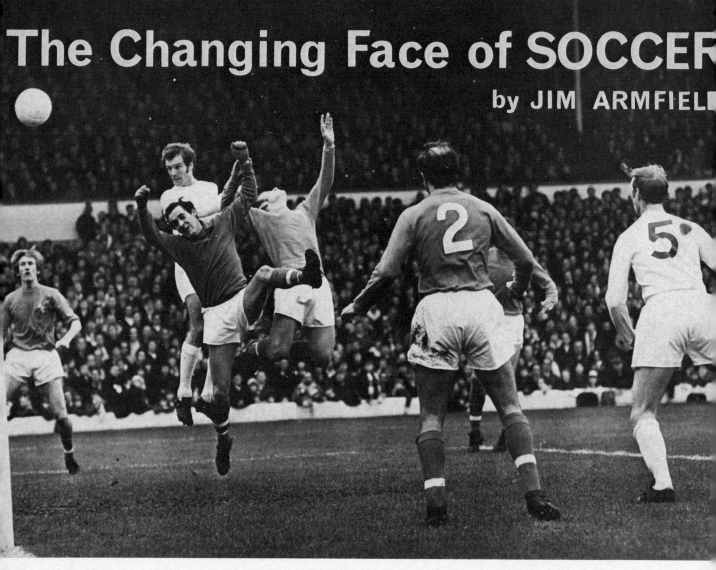

Football in the seventies—Leeds attacking the Blackpool goal and their two white-shirted players are 'defenders' Paul Madeley and Jack Charlton. Jim Armfield is Blackpool's No. 2

(1) The clothes we wore . . .

THE TREND TODAY IS FOR PLAYERS TO BE CAPABLE OF DOING THE JOBS OF ANY OTHER COLLEAGUE IN THE TEAM

JUST before last Christmas the girls were being persuaded by fashion designers to step out of their minis and dress up in the midis. Critics, mostly men, said it was putting the clock back twenty years or more. Come with me . . . twenty years back to when I first started in football . . . and you will see that we wore midis on the football field!

You will have seen pictures of players in those days, so you know what I mean. Shorts went down to the knees and the elastic at the top was so high that the waistline was almost under the chest! Shirts had collars with button sleeves, like a cricket

Flash-back to the long shorts of the players—and ballboy! Prostrate Bolton defenders watch Perry's shot go wide of the goal

shirt, and were made of fine wool. Socks were woollen, too, and we all wore boots with proper ankle cover and hammered in our three-nail studs.

In many ways the boots and socks gave more protection in tackles, but as fashion changed in the street so did our gear in football.

I remember as early as 1953 when Blackpool won the F.A. Cup after beating Bolton Wanderers, our players had special satin shorts for the occasion . . . and when they ran out at Wembley they got wolf whistles from the crowd! Since then shorts have got shorter, boots are lighter in all-plastic, studs are plastic and screwed in . . . and the socks are thinner with a blend of nylon in the wool.

There is, of course, a purpose for these changes . . . not a whim of fashion. Lighter and shorter strip gives more freedom of movement. Athletes today, for instance, wear shorts so brief that they have no legs. Plastic boots are designed to prevent holding too much mud.

And screw-in studs are a big help for swift changes for the whole team during bad weather when the pitch can vary from bone-hard to mud, or to ice and snow in a week of winter's worst conditions. Teams travelling away, for instance, can make late changes of studs after inspecting the pitch an hour before the kick-off.

The ball has changed, too. The old style all-leather ones have been replaced by more modern materials to prevent picking up moisture and mud which, in the old days, often made a ball weigh a pound heavier by the end of the game. The heavier ball had some advantages, however. I reckon it was easier to control, though it was heavier when heading. In fact the only time I have ever 'seen stars' when getting a ball in the face was years ago when Arsenal's Don Roper slammed a tremendous shot which struck me on the goal-line.

The new-type football boot came originally from West Germany and many players today still wear German-made ones. But I prefer the English boot.

(Above) *Blackpool won the 1953 Final—'Matthews' final—and here Stan receives his medal from the Queen watched by the then F.A. Secretary, Sir Stanley Rous*

(Below) *A close-up of the solid football boots of the fifties—as worn by the injured Nat Lofthouse and referee Griffiths*

Into the sixties—November 1962 to be more precise and, with some exceptions, there is still plenty of leg to the shorts. Spurs were attacking Glasgow Rangers' goal in the Cup-Winners Cup

(2) More wages, fewer faces . . .

When I first started at Blackpool I had to share a peg in the dressing-room! The club had over forty full-time professional players, and looking back, I can't think how we got into the changing rooms on training days. Today, with only twenty-five full timers, the dressing-rooms always seem full. At one time Blackpool turned out four teams on a Saturday with all paid players. But those were the days of maximum wages and the biggest change in soccer during my time came in 1960 when the restriction on wages was lifted. It had then reached £20 a week, with a bonus for winning and drawing. Today some players in wealthy city clubs are reputed to be earning ten times as much.

But they are the fortunate ones. For the average player the wage with bonuses has just about doubled. The increase, however, has been great enough to cause criticism. Hard-up clubs complain about the extra cost, but there is a far deeper effect taking place. Clubs everywhere are reducing the number of full-time professionals on their staffs and, compared with the old days, there are fewer chances for a young player to make his way in the game. It will get more difficult, too. One day we may see many clubs with only a first team squad and no professional reserve teams, as on the Continent where the famous Real Madrid operate this way.

I would like to stress at this point that it is more important than ever for young lads to train for an ordinary career while still trying to win a place in soccer. Most clubs encourage this and go out of their way to help a lad in vocational training in addition to lavishing a lot of money, time and patience in the effort to make him a fine footballer.

I mentioned money. Yes, clubs are spending a lot more on all aspects of the game. Grounds are being improved. The war halted a lot of development, but now the

15

The Yugoslavian Soskic saves from Jimmy Greaves in the F.I.F.A. XI v. England match in October 1963

wealthier clubs are building fine stadia with the accent on more seats and more cover. In the old days the majority of clubs had just a main stand and three sides for standing, most of it open to the skies.

And money is being spent on better training and medical facilities. Many clubs now have a training ground away from the stadium. Some even have indoor pitches and all the medical facilities so that a team need not see the stadium from one Saturday to the next. At Blackpool we used to train on a hired pitch to save wear-and-tear on the stadium ground during bad weather.

The result today is that pitches are in a far better condition for most of the nine months of the season. A lot of money has been spent by clubs who now have medical rooms that look like hospital units, sauna baths and expensive equipment for other forms of treatment . . . all in a bid to get injured players fit quicker. With so many more midweek matches there is a great urgency over injured players.

January 1971—and here's Jimmy Greaves in action for West Ham against Blackpool—Jim Armfield and keeper Taylor

(3) Money . . . and problems

Backstage there has been a big change. There are still managers who manage the club as well as the first team, but in the bigger clubs there is a tendency now to give the work to two men, calling one general manager and the other team 'boss'. This has been brought about by the growth of activities in the club for raising money and countless extra duties that occupy so much of one man's time that he hasn't enough to spare for giving close attention to the players. With a separate team manager the players have a man who sees everything that goes on in their training and coaching. He is a track-suit manager, which is what the term implies . . . a man who is out there with his players every day of the week . . . not leaving it to his trainer and coach.

Another big change has been the vital one of raising money for the clubs through outside activities. Greater emphasis has been placed on the development associations and supporters' clubs, for it is a true but sad fact that the vast majority of the Football League's ninety-two clubs would be in a sorry state without pools, raffles and other ideas to get extra money. For so many clubs these days the attendance 'turnstile cash' is

The verve and athleticism of today's players shown by Francis Lee in action for Manchester City

not enough to pay their way.

In fact, if soccer was run like a business looking for profit there would be an awful lot of closing down notices on the doors of clubs. Only the fanatical determination of directors and fans keep many clubs alive today.

So if you are asked to buy something from the club shop, a golden-shot ticket or a special brochure . . . remember, the club . . . your club . . . needs your money.

We all know that the big city clubs attract attendances of over 40,000, but for many clubs in smaller towns there has been a drifting away of the soccer population due to the change in habits, like other things, of a man and lad on a Saturday afternoon. In an effort to stimulate interest matches are televised, with payment, of course, to the Football League who share out the cash among all the clubs. TV has no doubt helped to make household names of many players who live far from the area of the local fan.

So much so that a regular fan doesn't need the number of a shirt to recognise a star in the visiting team.

There has also been masses of publicity in the form of books like this one, weekly magazines and increased effort in the newspapers to add colour and interest to our national game.

More players write their own columns. Some even have agents to help run their business affairs, for many on high wages are widely investing in businesses for the day when they retire.

I believe there is a problem facing the game on TV. It is appreciated that the elderly and sick need TV to see any football at all, but too many games on the 'telly' is a danger. Instead of them being something to urge people to see it 'live' there could develop a habit of relying on TV. Too much killed baseball attendances in the United States. I reckon one match a week is sufficient.

18

(4) The value of coaching

When I first started as a young professional, football was more or less played off the cuff. Generally speaking, footballers were born not made and our main job during the week in those days was to train hard for peak fitness and stamina. We were not given a lot of special coaching and it took me a few years to get to know what the game was all about. Nowadays the youngsters are told with lectures and demonstrations. Tactical formations are worked out with things to do in certain situations. It doesn't mean the game can be won by plotting it all on a blackboard, but it helps to provide a stronger defence, play on weaknesses known to exist in the other side and generally improve the pattern of team work . . . which, after all, is what the game really is all about. Individual brilliance, of course, goes a long way to getting the goals, but behind the approach work is usually a solid pattern of hard work, running to help attack and to defend . . . and ideally all of it organised so that each member of the team understands what the others are trying to do.

Years ago there was a tendency to sneer at coaching and one man, Mr. Walter Winterbottom, worked hard to get it accepted. This man, who was also England team manager for a long time (I don't know how he found the time to do two big jobs), slaved to get coaching properly established all over the country. The F.A. coaching centre at Lilleshall became a geographically central point in England for regular coaching courses. Footballers were invited to attend, even if they were stars who appeared to have expert knowledge. Some even failed the course! Others openly criticised it, but in the end commonsense prevailed, plus the persistence and patience of Mr. Winterbottom who was officially director of coaching for the F.A.

He had seen the trend towards proper coaching on the Continent. England, despite having many famous names in the team, had not done well in the World Cup. In the

A bounding youthful Bobby Moore in Chile 1962

1950 competition they even lost 1–0 to a United States team, a day of shame that was to be beaten later when the famous Hungarians, led by Ferenc Puskas, thrashed our lads 6–3 at Wembley in November 1953, and 7–1 in Hungary in May 1954.

But by 1961 England had produced what I thought was their best team for years. Yet in the following year when the World Cup was in Chile some changes were enforced through injury and sickness. However, we still did better than any other England squad in previous tourneys, going out to the eventual winners, Brazil, in the quarter finals.

The improvement in England's displays was echoed by the top clubs in the land. They went into the three major European

The end of an era? Sir Stanley Matthews comes out for his last match against an International XI at Stoke in April 1965

tournaments and the knowledge and experience of other nations and their ideas on how to play soccer became invaluable. Success of any team, whether at club or international level, leads to a great deal of copying by other clubs. Standards of play and fitness increased and when 1966 came round England really showed the world by winning the Jules Rimet Cup at Wembley. Sir Alf Ramsey had taken over three years before as England team manager, but Walter Winterbottom had, after his retirement, seen the fruits of his labours . . . rewards which spread throughout the country and brought international fame to England at last.

By now nearly every club in the Football League had a coach as well as trainer and players expected to be coached at training sessions. Tactical formations altered. Up to 1959 the 2–3–5 system was mostly favoured with players marking their opposite numbers . . . like right-half against inside-left, and so on.

Today only the goalkeepers 'stay at home'. We have the overlapping full-backs, the defender known as the 'sweeper' who covers for others at the back, wingers who sometimes play a special defensive role, deep-lying centre-forwards, two 'strikers' and systems which expect every outfield player to be able to work in any part of the field. Tactical formations are now called 4–2–4, 4–3–3 (England's in 1966) and 4–4–2. The Italians had these highly developed defensive tactics as early as the 50s and we used to criticise them. Now we have learned and adapted from them.

Football was slower in the old days and the standard of fitness was not so high, but the passing was every bit as good. Players specialised a lot more in certain positions and there were not so many 'utility' players. There were plenty of good wingers, like Stan Matthews, Tom Finney, Bobby Mitchell, Johnny Hancocks, Jimmy Mullen, Bryan Douglas . . . to mention only a few. I started as a right-winger, had the odd game at wing-half and centre-half and just one match at centre-foward after which I was never asked to play there again. In that match I reckon I had got two kicks . . . both on my right leg!

But the trend today is for players to be capable of doing the jobs of any other colleague in the team. Forwards are expected to tackle like defenders, full-backs must run and centre like wingers. Centre-halves even score from corners and free kicks and the attackers constantly inter-change. Part of the defensive tactics now is to funnel back under pressure and to put yourself between the ball and your goal to help form a wall of protection. It isn't wise to be beaten in a tackle and be temporarily out of the game. Defending players—and that includes forwards—must chase back. And that is my final spot of advice to youngsters in the game. Learn to play all the positions. You will be a much better player and know more about football.

Three Middlesbrough defenders group to try to stop the progress of George Best

MIKE ENGLAND····

A WORLD CLASS PLAYER

by JOE ROYLE

Joe Royle

MIKE ENGLAND HAS SOME TERRIFIC ATTRIBUTES—GREAT POWER IN THE AIR, AND THE HEIGHT TO USE HIS HEADING ABILITY TO THE BEST ADVANTAGE

THERE are a lot of very good centre-halves around in the First Division today; but, for my money Mike England, of Tottenham Hotspur, is the one who commands the greatest respect from me, as an opponent.

In the past, I have linked Mike's name with that of Ron Yeats of Liverpool, and Everton's Brian Labone. Well, big Ron and I may well duel no more, for Larry Lloyd seems to have established himself in the No. 5 jersey for Liverpool—and I haven't played enough against Larry yet to formulate judgment.

As for Brian Labone, I can speak only from what I have seen of him as a teammate, and I believe he has been one of the greatest centre-halves of the last decade in

Joe Royle in action for Everton against Chelsea

(Above) *Alan Ball with the Football Association Charity Shield after the reigning champions Everton had beaten Chelsea, the 1970 F.A. Cup holders*

(Left) *Two great headers of the ball in a duel—Mike England and Wyn Davies. Often, of course, team-mates in the Welsh national eleven*

British football. But when I look around the First Division now, as another season gets under way, I cannot escape the conclusion that it will be Mike England who gives me my hardest time of it, yet again.

The first time I played against him, I was little more than a kid. I didn't make much impression upon the giant Welshman—maybe I was somewhat overawed. But as I have gained in experience, I have come to appreciate that you need to be on top form to cope with this fellow.

I have another memory of Mike—a happier one than that of my first outing against him. It is of the occasion Everton met Tottenham at Goodison, when we were heading for the First Division Championship two seasons ago.

I really felt on form that day—and, even if it was indirectly, I contributed towards our 3–2 victory. I laid on the pass which brought our first goal, from Alan Whittle.

Not only that, but Mike England was penalised twice for fouls on me—and each time it meant a penalty. I didn't take either spot-kick: Alan Ball got the job, He scored

25

Happy days for Harry Catterick (holding the trophy) *and the Everton players after they had clinched the 1970 League Championship*

from one, missed the other.

And so the score stood at 2–2, with the minutes ticking away and our need for two points becoming all the more urgent. Then I got the ball and slotted it into the net, to score the winner.

Last season, as Tottenham challenged for the honours, I feel that big Mike had his best season since he joined them from Blackburn Rovers, until he was injured.

For me, he has always been a tremendously talented player—what you can truly call a footballing centre-half. Some folk have been known to observe that Mike tries to play too much football at times—that he will do it in his own penalty area, when the big boot would be better.

I don't go along with this school of thought for I can honestly say that Mike has never given me any openings through fiddling about with the ball in his team's danger zone.

He has some terrific attributes—great power in the air, and the height to use his heading ability to the best advantage. I really have to pull out all the stops when it's an aerial duel between us.

Not only is Mike a commanding figure in the air—despite his size he is far from cumbersome. There's nothing slow or sluggish about the Tottenham defender.

I've heard it said, too, that he is not physically hard enough, considering his size . . . but the people who have criticised him on this score obviously haven't played directly against him! Certainly he is not a dirty player (despite those two penalties!), but I have felt the full impact of Mike's weight on more than one occasion.

Mike England, in my view, HAS put a little bit more steel into his play—and he is less tempted, these days, to go venturing upfield. Although, when an attacking move is really on, he will go forward; and, because of his great ability to play pure football, he has every reason for doing so.

Mike began his league career with Blackburn, of course, and during his time with the Rovers he proved that he could play in several positions, including attack.

Indeed, there seemed to be a time when he might be destined to make a name for himself as a scoring forward, but eventually he was recognised as a centre-half of rare class and power.

Tottenham Hotspur paid Blackburn £95,000 for Mike, in the summer of 1966. I reckon that had he been born in England, he would have played in the World Cup.

As it was, Tottenham decided that he was the man to do the centre-half job for them, and it is a tremendous tribute to his ability that he has been their automatic choice for the No. 5 jersey, barring injury.

I've heard and read a lot about the great John Charles, who could play at centre-half or centre-forward with equal distinction. Some people reckoned it was a pity that there weren't TWO John Charles. Then Wales would have had a scoring centre-forward and an impassable centre-half!

I reckon that Mike England is the natural successor to John Charles—he gives you the feeling that here is a player of true class. And I do mean WORLD class.

Coming from someone who spends 180 minutes every season trying to get the better of Mike England, I reckon that's a tribute, indeed. And, as a centre-forward whose job it is to get goals, I'm glad to pay due respect to the opponent I rate the greatest.

But I can promise big Mike one thing—this season, as ever, I'll be out to put one across him!

Dennis Bond, Joe Royle and Phil Beal in action at Goodison Park

David Sadler with the European Champions Cup after Manchester United's Final win over Benfica

FROM STRIKER TO SWEEPER
by David Sadler

Peter Shilton, Brian Kidd, Ralph Coates, Peter Thompson, David Sadler and Bob McNab in Ecuador prior to the 1970 World Cup matches. If they look a bit disappointed it is because they have learned they are the 'six' who had to be pared from the touring party to reduce to the nominated W.C. '22'. But there is always tomorrow . . .

. . . HERE AM I, A PLAYER WHO WAS SIGNED TO SCORE GOALS, NOW BEING CAST IN THE ROLE OF STOPPER

IT has often been said that there is no short cut to success in professional football—but there can be accidents of fate which give a player's career a sudden twist . . . for better or for worse. A twist of fate such as happened to me, for instance.

It may sound as if I'm getting on a bit, when I go back to my days with Isthmian

29

Gary Sprake safely collects the ball above Willie Morgan's head watched by Terry Cooper and George Best

League club Maidstone, for I was playing for them in the early 1960s; but, in fact, I was a youngster then. Indeed, I'm only in my middle 20s now.

But at that time, I was playing a striker's role, at inside-forward—and for two seasons in succession I finished up as Maidstone's top scorer. And so it came about that the big professional clubs began to take an interest in me.

I found myself reading stories that this club and that club were rivals for my signature, that I was rated as a potential England centre-forward. All very nice to read . . . but even then, I wasn't taking anything for granted.

However, it turned out that quite a number of crack clubs HAD been taking notice of my scoring form, and ultimately, Manchester United were the club who came along and persuaded me to sign amateur forms for them. That was in November 1962.

I didn't go up to Old Trafford straight away—I continued to play for Maidstone until I was 17, in February 1963. And then I became a professional footballer with Manchester United.

I'll admit it—I really believed that they were signing me to groom me as a striker. And I have no doubt that United themselves thought that they were investing in a youngster who had the potential to score goals in League soccer.

I arrived at Old Trafford and I began trying to win my spurs as a scorer of goals; eventually, I found myself promoted to the first team.

But it didn't take me long to learn that what I had suspected was true—it isn't a smooth path to the top in the professional game, and there can be moments when you have doubts about it all.

I found myself in and out of the first team, a player who made a few goals, scored a few—but one who couldn't say with any sort of certainty that he had arrived to stay.

I was still young, of course—in fact, I was eligible to play for United's under-20 team, which around that time took part in an annual soccer tournament in Switzerland. I went twice on tour with the United youngsters—and the second time we ran into real injury trouble when two players had to drop out.

It meant that United had no centre-half and no cover for the position. So I was asked to give it a go in the No. 5 jersey. I wasn't quite a stranger to the role, for in training I had played defensively several times.

I did pretty well as a centre-half, too, and United won the tournament. But at the start of the following season, I was back again as an inside-forward.

However, later on I was tried out again as a centre-half—and I got into the first team in this position. Gradually, people began to look upon me more as a defensive player, rather than a forward striker.

And now, of course, I have developed the defensive role, until I am regarded as a sweeper.

There is one thing about having played both roles—attacker and defender—and that is you are more aware of what is likely to be going through an opposing forward's mind, when your rivals are on the attack.

So you may be able to read situations that little bit quicker; and your anticipation can help you to make timely interventions.

At the same time, this game of soccer is changing so quickly, even season by season, that you have to learn to adjust and adapt yourself to the many facets of the game.

For instance, midfield play has become a dominating factor—take Everton, for example: they have three of the greatest midfield men in the business in Ball, Harvey and Kendall. AND they spent £150,000 on another midfield man, when they signed Henry Newton from Nottingham Forest . . . yet last season he played at left-back.

Remember, too, that Bobby Charlton became famed as a player with a cannon-ball shot—a man who could almost blast the net when he hammered the ball for goal. Yet in the past few seasons, Bobby has become a midfield mastermind.

As I said, the changing nature of the game itself often means that a player has to adapt himself to a new role. And here am I, a player who was signed to score goals, now being cast in the role of stopper.

Had anyone told me, on the day I left Maidstone for Old Trafford, that I would end up by winning recognition from England team-manager Sir Alf Ramsey as a centre-half, I should probably have laughed in disbelief.

In fact, I have to admit that I wasn't over-impressed when I read, a few seasons ago, that Sir Matt Busby was tipping me to play for England at centre-half.

And today? Well, I recognise that I AM

David Sadler in an attacking role outjumps Mike England

a candidate for the next World Cup tournament . . . and as a No. 5.

I also recognise that I have developed a certain defensive ability, and that a footballer has to play to his strengths.

By choice, I suppose, I would still rather be a dashing striker, a man who hits the headlines because he's knocking in the goals —but you won't find me grumbling because I'm wearing a defender's jersey these days.

The strikers, they say, take the knocks, but I can assure you they don't take all of them!

As for me, I'm satisfied to be holding down a first-team place at what is still one of the greatest clubs in the world. If luck goes my way, I'll win further honours at representative level.

Whichever way it goes, I've still come a long way—even in a roundabout fashion—since I was sticking the ball into the net for Maidstone.

The Reign of Leeds

BY STAN LIVERSEDGE

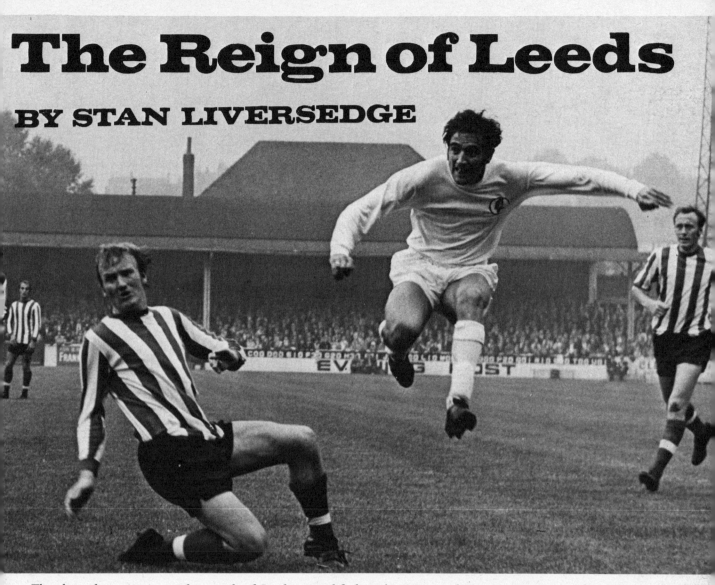

The sheer determination and strength of Leeds exemplified in this picture of Norman Hunter attacking against Southampton

WHO WOULD DARE TO SAY THAT LEEDS UNITED ARE COMING TO THE END OF THEIR DAYS AT THE TOP?

HOW long will the reign of Leeds United continue? That is one question which must be looming large in the mind of manager Don Revie, as a new season gets under way.

Leeds, undoubtedly, have been the team of the late 60s—they came from Second Division obscurity to win promotion, finish as First Division runners-up twice in quick succession, and as losing F.A. Cup Finalists at Wembley. Then they really began to lose their reputation of being the best second-besters in the business. . . .

Leeds went to Wembley again, and collected the League Cup, after their duel

Not much chance here for Manchester City's Alan Oakes with Johnny Giles, Billy Bremner and Jack Charlton in attendance!

with Arsenal; they added the European Fairs Cup to their list of honours, and finished with a flourish by winning the First Division Championship, with a record haul of points.

All this is history of the late 1960s, of course; and so is the fact that Leeds United became the unluckiest treble-chancers ever, when they missed out on the European Cup, the F.A. Cup and the First Division title, in season 1969–70.

But through these years of success—and the season of that near-miss when they went for the treble—Leeds United emerged, above all, as the team that just didn't lose. Well, hardly ever, any way.

Two defeats in the season when they won the title with 67 points; and only half a dozen in the season which saw them come second to Everton.

Only a couple of seasons or so ago, Don Revie told me: 'I think we've proved that we have got a fine side now—but I reckon we'll be even better when the average age of the team is around 27.

'The younger players in the side will have

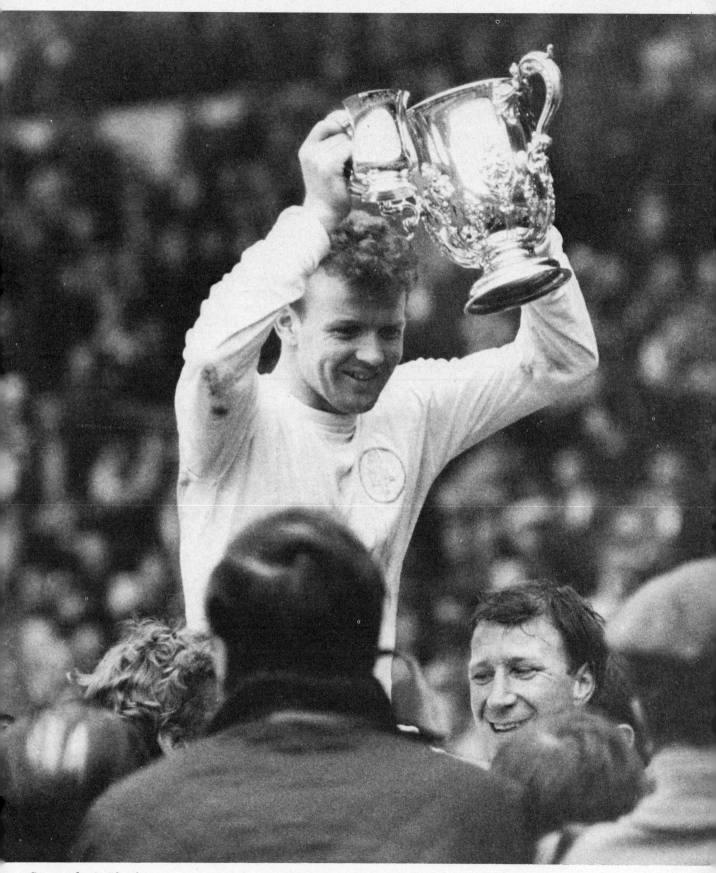

Success for Leeds after so many near-misses—Billy Bremner holds the Cup aloft after Leeds' win over Arsenal in the 1968 League Cup Final

The familiar sight of big Jack Charlton galloping upfield—or hastening back to defence!

Mick Jones

Peter Lorimer

matured by then, and we have so many youngsters that they can only improve.'

Today, the average age of Leeds United IS around 27—and they are poised once more to make a strong bid for all the honours going. But how long can they retain their near-supremacy?

This is the jackpot question, for even while a team is at its peak, and playing well enough to win almost every game, let alone draw, that team's manager must be looking to the future.

Harry Catterick of Everton once told me that he was always planning five years ahead; Bill Shankly of Liverpool told me that he had foreseen the break-up of his great side of the 60s.

Bill admitted that he thought his all-conquering team would have lasted a little bit longer, before he had to draft in replacements. But, even so, he was buying wisely, just in case. . . .

And when the time came for a major injection of new blood, players like Ray Clemence, Larry Lloyd and John Mc-Laughlin were ready to be pitched into the fray.

Leeds are not an old side, now—their

Terry Cooper and Jimmy Johnstone in a Leeds-Celtic European Cup semi-final

veteran, of course, is big Jackie Charlton, who is in his mid-30s. But, nevertheless, players like Billy Bremner, Norman Hunter, Johnny Giles—all key men—are one year older.

At the same time, these players are well on the right side of 30—and men like Gary Sprake, Paul Reaney, Terry Cooper, Paul Madeley, Allan Clarke, Mick Jones, Peter Lorimer and Eddie Gray are still only nudging the mid-20s.

What does Revie say now, about his team? 'Well, I believe that we should be just about reaching our peak—and that we should be able to maintain our standard for two or three years.

'Indeed, we can get better still . . . provided everyone remembers that it is always necessary to keep on working, and keep on learning.'

Clearly, then, anyone who reckons that Leeds are going to go over the hill, any time now, is not thinking along the same lines as the United manager.

He agrees with Harry Catterick about planning five years ahead, though—'I think he's absolutely right . . . we try to plan five years ahead at Elland Road, too,' says Revie.

Has he got the talent already coming along in the reserves, against the time when replacements are required for established stars? 'You can only tell when a player is pitched into the top flight,' says the Leeds boss. But he adds: 'So far, the lads who have been pitched in have proved that they can make it . . . and I'm optimistic about the youngsters who are waiting in the wings now.'

Last season, as Leeds were pushing on

towards their title goal, Revie was asked how many players were necessary for a first-team pool. He gave his answer—about twenty.

He also handed out a generous measure of praise to midfield general Johnny Giles. And so did Arsenal manager Bertie Mee.

Giles always was a fine little footballer—but since he left Manchester United for Leeds he has become a star in his own right.

What brought about this transformation? Revie sums it up simply enough: 'Responsibility . . . I think that, more than anything, has helped to make Johnny a great player.

'He always did have ability; he could read a situation, could pass a ball tremendously accurately. But the responsibility he was given here brought the best out of him.

'Johnny took the chance with both hands; he revelled in the opportunity to show that he could shoulder responsibility. And today, he is recognised as a key player.'

Some of the men of Leeds United seem to have been around for many a year now—Billy Bremner, for instance, and Jackie Charlton. Yet Charlton is still the only man in his mid-30s—the rest have yet to reach that one-time age 'barrier'.

Remembering that players like Bremner have been at Elland Road virtually since they left school; remembering that Leeds are just coming up to that average age of 27; and remembering that Revie, planning ahead, is nothing, if not thorough . . . who would dare say that Leeds United are coming to the end of their days at the top? Certainly not me!

Pat Jennings (grounded) *and Cyril Knowles combine to keep Billy Bremner at bay*

Two fine midfield players seem to be sharing a joke—but maybe not with each other! John Hollins and Bobby Charlton

A THANKLESS JOB···SOMETIMES
by John Hollins

You can't see John Hollins in this picture but it was his powerful leg that sent this thundering shot past Southampton's Eric Martin for a Chelsea goal

CHAPS WHO PLAY MY ROLE ARE REGULARLY ACCUSED OF EITHER BEING FAR TOO ATTACK-CONSCIOUS OR TOO DEFENCE-MINDED

THE job of a midfield worker-cum-schemer-cum-goalscorer can on many occasions be a thankless one.

Chaps who play my role are regularly accused of either being far too attack-conscious or too defence-minded. So, as you can see from what I have already stated, sometimes you simply cannot win.

During the past twelve months, however, I think I have conquered many of my previous failings. In other words, I am now much more selective when I go forward and have a bang at goal. And as such I am now scoring more goals than ever before. In fact, my goal against Arsenal during the match at Stamford Bridge at the beginning of the 1970–71 season was voted by the Fulham Road fans as the best they had ever seen.

This was a great honour as far as I was concerned considering that I came above

At last—it took a replay at Old Trafford to do it but skipper Ron Harris, with cup, and his mates can celebrate Chelsea's 1970 F.A. Cup win over Leeds

blokes such as Jimmy Greaves, Bobby Tambling and Peter Osgood in the poll.

Apart from this honour, I have once again caught the eye of England manager Sir Alf Ramsey. So with luck I can look forward to playing for my country in the 1974 World Cup in Munich.

This next World Cup could well be the most interesting tactically. After Brazil's almost cavalier-style forward play in the 1970 World Finals, a great many people were quick to predict that countries such as England, West Germany, Italy and Russia would attempt to adopt a similar approach.

The 1970 World Cup Final—and a clash of national styles between Brazil's attacking flair and Italy's defensive strength with non-football weather adding a further twist to the story

Frankly, I don't know what will happen in the next few years. The England team, for some seasons the 4–4–2 supremos, were very quick to change to the more fluid 4–3–3 system for the first full international after the defeat in Mexico.

Does this mean, therefore, that a new tidal wave of frantic attacking soccer will dominate our game? Or will ourselves, West Germany and Italy continue to put greater emphasis on defence, relying on quick breakaways?

Being a careful chap, as far as forecasting the future is concerned I suppose that eventually we could reach a balance stage—a sort of mixture of both ideologies.

The obvious fact is, however, that in Brazil and to a lesser extent Peru, they breed forwards in the mode of Georgie Best, Charlie Cooke, Rodney Marsh and Peter Osgood like rabbits.

In fact, everyone out there craves to be an attacking forward, the job of a goalkeeper is almost entirely reserved for a chap with a wooden leg!

But in Italy, soccer borders on almost defence-mania. The young kids basically admire hard tackling, and the plan there is simply to keep your goal intact, hoping for a breakaway (dare I say a lucky one) to score the killer-punch goal.

We have certainly not reached that stage in England. But we still seem to breed numerous world-class defenders and midfield dynamos at the expense of the artistic player who is so often literally kicked or intimidated out of a match.

Certainly a team with our defence and the Brazilian forwards would be completely unbeatable!

Bobby Moore

ARE CAPTAINS BORN OR MADE?

wonders BOBBY MONCUR

A fine tackle by the stripe-shirted Bobby Moncur halts a Wolves attack

... WHILE THE GAME IS GOING ON, THERE ARE TIMES WHEN A CAPTAIN HAS TO THINK QUICKLY BEFORE DECIDING WHAT TO DO OR SAY ...

ARE captains born—or made? That's a question I've pondered more than once since I became the skipper of Newcastle United. And I've come to the conclusion that, in the final analysis, it's a bit of both.

Anyone who has been a soccer fan will recall that Newcastle United had a tremendous team during the 1950s—they had

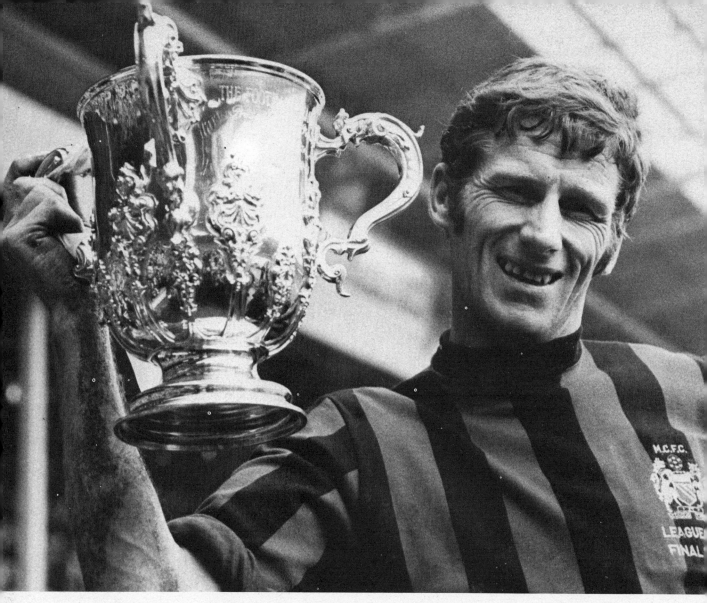

A happy club captain—Tony Book with the trophy after Manchester City won the 1970 F.L. Cup Final

players like 'Wor Jackie' Milburn, the Robledo brothers, wee Ernie Taylor, big Frank Brennan, Bobby Mitchell and . . . Joe Harvey.

Joe was one of the greatest skippers of all time—a big, craggy defender who inspired his team-mates, who cajoled, shouted and got the best out of them. Now Joe Harvey is the manager of Newcastle United—and he has scored another success in this role.

When Newcastle were going through their palmy days of the 1950s, I was still a lad—I hail from Perth, in Scotland, and I was attending Broxburn High School. Of course, I wanted to become a professional footballer.

I was lucky enough to be chosen for the Scottish Boys side—George Graham, now with Arsenal, and Jim Forrest, one-time of Rangers and Preston—were team-mates of mine then.

I confess that I did begin to wonder if a soccer career was for me, though, because I had trials with Manchester United, Wolves and Preston, before Newcastle came along to say: 'We want you.'

Oddly enough, when Newcastle won the F.A. Youth Cup, Wolves were the team we defeated in the Final . . . and I was the one who scored the winning goal. I'll admit it—I enjoyed playing an attacking role, as a wing-half; but even so early in my

Everton's skipper Alan Ball in action

footballing career, I learned one lesson from 'the boss'. For Joe Harvey gently pointed out to me that if I thought of nothing but going upfield on attacking forays, then I would be leaving a gap in defence.

Gradually, then, I learned to become a more defensive player, at left-half—although when I finally broke through to the first team, I made my debut at centre-half. That was eight years ago, now, at Luton.

But four more years were to pass before I could say: 'I've arrived.' It was 1967 by the time I had made the No. 6 spot my own in Newcastle's first team.

Only a year after that, I had won my first Under-23 cap for Scotland, and been awarded my first full International cap. I felt that I was really on the way up.

But, of course, it was when I became skipper of Newcastle four seasons ago that I really began to realise that I had responsibilities not only to myself, but to the rest of the team and to the club.

I was honoured by being chosen as skipper, but I felt that I had to do more than just play my best, to live up to the role. Consequently, I was driving, urging, shouting, coaxing—and sometimes forgetting a little thing called psychology.

In the seasons since I first became Newcastle's skipper, I believe I have improved, year by year.

I have listened to advice many times from 'the boss'—I haven't always agreed with him, and sometimes I have argued my point of view—but I have come to realise that, often enough, the manager can see the overall picture better, even, than the skipper.

Aggression is a good quality to have, on the field of play, but you can't always adopt the same attitude when the game is over.

And while the game is going on, there are times when a captain has to think quickly, before deciding what to do or say. This is where that psychology touch comes in, as I have come to appreciate.

Some players respond to a bit of shouting, others tend to take it to heart, and the reaction is just the reverse of what you had

Ron Harris, captain of Chelsea

intended. Instead of getting the extra effort you find that you've made someone retreat into a shell.

So as my experience has increased, I have come to know when to shout, and when not to shout; when to encourage, and when to try to inspire by example.

People have been kind enough to say that I'm a good captain—I have even been compared with 'the boss'. But I know, and Joe Harvey knows, that I haven't learned ALL the arts and crafts of captaincy, even yet.

I HAVE learned patience, tolerance, and the need for studying my team-mates. I have also learned the need to take a long, hard look at myself, on occasion. And all this, I believe, has made me a better skipper as time has gone by.

Some people, they say, are born leaders, others will lead when they have responsibility thrust upon them.

I sometimes feel that I am a mixture of both—I enjoy being the skipper of the team, and I lead because I have had the responsibility put upon my shoulders.

Certainly I never considered that I had been born to lead, or that leadership was mine by right. Yet I have always been ready to step in and take the lead, if I have felt that the need for this has been there.

Perhaps, in the long run, you have to have that inborn feeling of wanting to lead, if you are handed the chance. But this is only part of the answer, as I now know.

Because I have discovered that a captain never knows it all, just as a manager never knows it all. You learn something from every game. And what you learn helps you to become a better skipper next time out.

You may be born with the instinctive ability to lead, to be a captain; but it's the use you make of the experience you gain, as you go along, which counts for a lot, too.

Bobby Moncur clears safely before Bobby Gould can strike

Tottenham's 4 National Team Captains

Maybe it was coincidence—maybe the influence of the club or perhaps of Danny Blanchflower—but within the space of a few seasons Tottenham have supplied captains of Northern Ireland (Blanchflower himself), Wales (Mike England seen in a tussle for the ball with Francis Lee),

Scotland (Dave Mackay seen playing for Derby against Chelsea) and England (Alan Mullery who deputised as skipper for Bobby Moore against Malta in February 1971)

A return to First Division football for ALL STARS editor, Jim Armfield, seen here challenging Leeds' Norman Hunter

GREEN FOR GO ··· AT LAST!
by Tony Green

WITH FULL TRAINING AGAIN I GOT MY MATCH FITNESS BACK AND, TO QUOTE AN OLD PUN THAT I HAVE HAD TO LIVE WITH, IT WAS 'GREEN FOR GO'

THE day was 27 July 1969. Time, about 11 a.m. The scene, Blackpool's training ground near the airport. I shall always remember it. That 'strain' I suddenly felt near the left ankle put me out of big-time football for a whole season.

The injury turned out to be the Achilles

Tony Coleman

tendon and instead of kicking off with the lads on 9 August I was to start a series of treatment that included an operation in Wrightington Hospital, near Wigan.

When I came out of hospital my leg was in plaster. After they took that off they put several thin layers of leather on to the heel of my left walking shoe. They gave me a stick and for weeks I walked about like an old man! Gradually the layers were removed one by one as my ankle was 'lowered' to the normal angle.

People ask me if I was depressed being out of the game all that time. Honestly, I can say no, because everyone was so kind to me and there is always a supreme air of optimism in football where every player has to take knocks both mentally and physically . . . and get up again. Injuries are part and

parcel of our game and we are used to spending a lot of time on the treatment table.

But I did miss playing. It was 'murder' having to be a spectator at Blackpool's matches, particularly as they were going strongly for promotion from Division Two after a couple of seasons 'down'. They made it by being runners-up to Huddersfield . . . without me!

I was also disappointed at the set-back because I had been in Scotland's international squad as substitute a couple of times, against Cyprus and Austria.

But patience and expert treatment were rewarded and I made my return to the game in a warm-up match in Northern Ireland before the start of the 1970–71 season. I was put on as substitute . . . and lasted THREE MINUTES!

It was only a calf muscle strain, but uninformed people started to write me off and there were some ominous headlines about me suggesting that I was finished as a player. But they were wrong.

After missing the first eight League games and a League Cup-tie I was substitute for the home game against Everton on 9 September. The 12th man job lasted 80 minutes because I was put on 10 minutes after the start when Tony Coleman fell heavily and injured his shoulder. I got through the game, but felt very tired . . . the expected reaction after being on the sidelines so long. In top class football today you have to be extremely fit and you soon notice a fall-off in your condition if you cannot train properly through injury.

Anyway, I was picked for the next game and lasted 75 minutes before another leg muscle 'went'. I was rested for three matches and then on my second 'comeback' I scored! With full training again I got my match fitness back and, to quote an old pun that I have had to live with, it was 'Green for Go!' If it is true that luck, the bad and the good, evens out over the years, I should be set to keep going from now on—to the top of the football ladder!

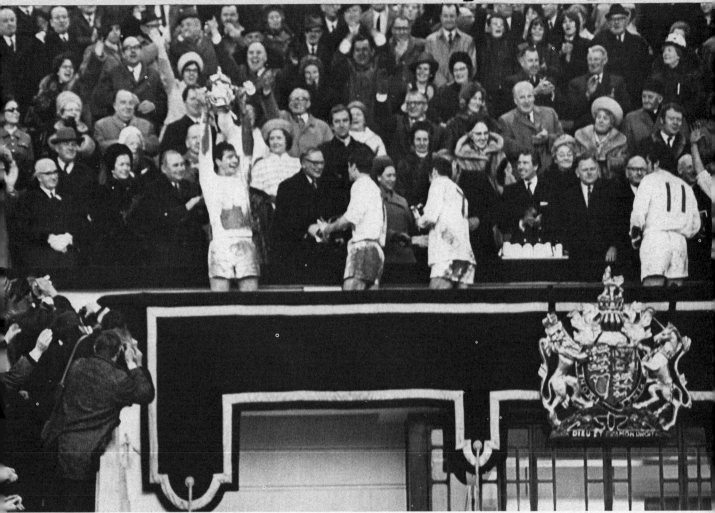

Swindon at Wembley—and the 1969 Football League Cup winners over Arsenal. Stan Harland holds the Cup aloft. Don Rogers is No. 11

BY STICKING TO SWINDON, I ACHIEVED TWO OF MY BIG AMBITIONS—TO PLAY AT WEMBLEY AND TAKE PART IN A EUROPEAN TOURNAMENT

IT'S no secret that I made many attempts to persuade Swindon Town to allow me a transfer. Being an ambitious person I had always set my heart on playing in the First Division and perhaps getting the chance to play in one of the big European competitions. But the club continually turned down my requests. Now, in one respect at least, I realise that was something of a blessing in disguise. For, by sticking with Swindon, I achieved two of my big ambitions—to play at Wembley, and take part in a European tournament.

I remember telling one reporter, after one of my transfer requests, that all the future held for me at Swindon was run-of-the-mill

Don Rogers

Third Division games plus the odd cup-tie. I told him that I couldn't remember any Third Division player ever gracing the Wembley turf, apart from Queen's Park Rangers in the League Cup—and that was one of those things which happened once in fifty years.

In my wildest dreams I couldn't have imagined that, within months of uttering those words, I would walk out on to the Wembley pitch with the Swindon lads!

The only thing that differed from my dream was 'the lush green turf' as I had always known it. That day, when we faced Arsenal in the 1969 League Cup Final, Wembley was a bit of a mud-heap. Worse than many of the Third Division pitches I had often complained about.

Never mind. It was Wembley. And that's something very special for any player. Particularly so for me because we pulled off one of the biggest surprises of the century by beating Arsenal 3–1 after extra-time—and I had the good fortune to score the two extra-time goals which gave us the trophy.

I always find I play better on the big occasion. Looking back over my career I have been able to pull out something special in most of our cup-ties and in my two Under-23 internationals for England. In my second, against Wales, I scored the winning goal. And I recall some good games against West Ham, when we knocked them out of the F.A. Cup, and several other of our giant-killing games.

It's something to do with the atmosphere. The big crowds, the tension before the game. It's all so different from the ordinary League match feeling. You get the sense of occasion. And I thrive on that.

That's why I always wanted to get into the First Division and experience that big-match occasion every week.

I've never had any complaint against the club. Swindon is a good club. They've treated me well. Nor is it to do with money. I simply love the game and wanted to play it at its highest level.

But, as I said, Swindon's refusals led to that Wembley Final and a crack at European competitive football. That year the Italian and English Leagues had arranged for the first match in an annual challenge between the League Cup winners in each country.

We travelled to meet Roma and lost 1–2 in the first leg. But we crushed them 4–0 in the return at Swindon, when I scored one of the goals, to claim the club's first success in Europe.

The following season we were invited to take part in another new competition—the Anglo-Italian tournament—in which several clubs from each country took part in a league tournament played on a home-and-away basis. The most successful club from each country were to meet in the Final.

Well, once again, Swindon came out on top! We had to play Naples on their own ground. And what a match that turned out to be!

Peter Noble scored twice, and Arthur Horsfield once, to put us into a 3–0 lead. The home crowd went mad at their own team, and as the game went on the atmosphere became very unpleasant. Spectators were ripping out the seats and throwing them, and stones, across the moat on to the pitch.

It was a sad thing because the game had been such a sporting one. But things got so bad that the referee finally had to abandon the game with 12 minutes to go and we were awarded the trophy.

And to think that the competition was organised to promote friendliness between the two countries!

It's funny in a way because that was the second time I had played an important match against an Italian club when the game couldn't be completed. On the previous occasion the game came to a premature end because our opponents suddenly took it into their heads to walk off the field.

When Swindon first gained promotion to Division Two in 1963 they were invited to enter an under-21 team for an inter-nation

One of the goals that sunk Arsenal in the 1969 League Cup Final. No doubt about the referee's decision! Don Rogers (11) was the scorer

competition in Belgium. Well, we won our way quite easily into the Final when our opponents were Torino.

During the game the referee gave a decision which they seemed to disagree with. They started to argue, then they chased the poor chap off the field. When the referee recovered to call for order the Italians had all gone off to the dressing-room and there was no alternative but to abandon the game.

I've been with Swindon since I was 15 and I've been playing in the first team for the past eight years. I've had many happy memories like those—at least, they're happy to look back on though they weren't necessarily funny at the time.

Another unforgettable moment in my career took place before I ever kicked a ball

for Swindon. It was the day I travelled from my home in the tiny village of Paulton, in Somerset, to sign for them—that was the first time in my life I had ever travelled on a train.

Since that day I've found the Swindon supporters wonderful folk. They've given me tremendous encouragement all the time. Once, when I asked for a transfer, many season-ticket holders threatened to resign if the club released me.

At the same time, I think the Swindon fans have always understood that I wanted to better myself by playing First Division football. But now that the club is established in Division Two there's quite a good chance that Swindon will themselves be a First Division club in the not-too-distant future.

MY FEET ARE ON THE GROUND
by LARRY LLOYD

Larry Lloyd guides the ball safely towards his keeper Ray Clemence as Arsenal's Ray Kennedy runs in

I'M STILL BUSY CONCENTRATING ON HOLDING DOWN MY FIRST-TEAM PLACE IN THE FIRST DIVISION WITH LIVERPOOL ... AS FOR 1974—WE'LL WAIT AND SEE

EVER since I was chosen to play for the England Under-23 team early last season, against West Germany and then against Sweden, people have been asking me what I think about my chances of winning full England honours and getting into the World Cup side for 1974.

Well, it's nice to know that people think you are good enough to be rated as having a CHANCE—but, to tell the honest truth, I just don't allow myself to look so far ahead.

Not because I haven't the confidence in myself, but simply because so many things can happen in football, over the space of two or three years. As I have experienced for myself, in just one short season!

A player can go through a spell when he is right out of touch, and I don't kid myself —this can happen to ANY footballer. Including me.

A player can sustain an injury which puts him out of action at a crucial time—maybe, even for many weeks. Colin Harvey of Everton will never know how much that eye-infection trouble cost him . . . did it rob him of the chance to go with England to Mexico, last time out?

Last season Bobby Graham broke an ankle, just at a time when he was hitting the headlines and being tipped for a Scottish cap. Luckily, my Liverpool team-mate wasn't out of action for more than a couple of months or so—but it could have been much worse.

And what about Peter Dobing and Willie Stevenson of Stoke? Each of these players broke a leg last season, and found themselves out of action for months. Yes, soccer fate can strike blows as suddenly as this.

I don't pretend to myself that I'm the ONLY centre-half who has come under the eye of Sir Alf Ramsey, either—Roy McFarland of Derby County, and Dennis Smith of Stoke are obviously candidates for international recognition.

And somewhere along the way, over the next couple of years, a youngster at present unknown may well emerge as a very real contender for the England No. 5 jersey.

So you'll see I'm keeping my feet planted firmly on the ground, when it comes to dreaming dreams of fame in 1974.

Yet, of course, I DO have ambition—any professional footballer must believe in himself enough to think that he can get right to the top. And things CAN happen fast in football.

There was I, playing for Third Division Bristol Rovers, with but fifty first-team games behind me, when out of the blue I'm

told: 'Liverpool want to sign you.' And when I heard the fee was £50,000, you could have knocked me down with a feather!

It didn't take long for me to decide I would go to Anfield, of course—although I knew that with Ron Yeats a fixture I might have to wait quite a while to stake my claim to a first-team place.

But I was young—I'm still only 22—and I knew that I could learn a lot with Liverpool. And I believe you HAVE to be ready to learn . . . you cannot afford to think you know it all, in this game.

Indeed, although I spent last season as a regular in Liverpool's first team—and that promotion came more quickly than I had ever expected—you might have noticed that I didn't go venturing upfield very often.

I felt that I should concentrate on mastering the job I had been given—which meant that I should gain all the experience possible of defensive play. After all, that was what I was wearing the No. 5 shirt for—to stop folk like Jeff Astle, Wyn Davies and Ron Davies putting the ball in Liverpool's net.

I learned one thing quickly, as I played against each of these stars—they're tremendously good, especially in the air, but they are fairly predictable.

I knew that they would be given a fair number of crosses, and—as I'm a six-footer myself—I knew also that I was in with a chance when we went up for the ball. That's how it worked out, by and large, too.

In my first three games against these heading aces, only Jeff Astle managed to get the ball in the net.

Frankly, I would rather tackle the orthodox type of centre-forward than the will-o'-the-wisp type like my team-mate Bobby Graham.

It's one thing to know you can stick close to a player, without having to wander too much from your 'patrol section'; it's another to find that the man you're supposed to be marking is popping up here, there and everywhere. You can be caught in two minds, then.

My first experience of coming up against

Ron Davies intent upon making powerful contact on the ball with his head

Everton's Joe Royle was before I had joined Liverpool—I played for Bristol Rovers in an F.A. Cup-tie at Goodison, and we lost 1–0.

Joe got the goal—not a header, but a shot —and so when I came up against him again, in the derby game last November at Anfield, I was prepared for an afternoon of real hard work.

I played for Bristol Rovers as an amateur

for a couple of years, while I was working as a fitter, and I didn't really start to think about turning professional until I got the chance of a first-team game in a Gloucester Senior Cup Final, against Bristol City.

Rovers' regular centre-half went down with flu, and I was called in to replace him. We lost, but I felt I hadn't done too badly, and when I had a chat with the manager about a career in football, he didn't hesitate about offering me professional terms.

That's how it all started . . . and after a full season as understudy to Ron Yeats at Liverpool, I broke into First Division football, found myself playing against top-class opposition week in, week out, was plunged into the European fray, and then won an England Under-23 cap.

So you'll see what I mean, when I say it all seemed to be happening at once. But as for 1974 . . . we'll wait and see. I'M still busy concentrating on holding down my first-team place in the First Division with Liverpool. And THAT will do for me to be going on with.

If I'm lucky, then other honours will follow.

Two minds with a single thought as Tommy Smith and Alan Gilzean keep their eyes on the ball

CLUBS THAT ARE ALWAYS GREAT-TO SOME

by Gordon Jeffery

I SUSPECT THAT MOST OF US, EVEN WHEN OUR LOYALTY IS TO MODEST, UNSUCCESSFUL, UNGLAMOROUS CLUBS, LIKE TO ENJOY SOME OF THE GLORY REFLECTED FROM A SUCCESSFUL CLUB

EVERY Monday morning during the football season, when an old friend of mine joins me about half-way through my train journey to London, he wants first to talk about what Bolton Wanderers had done on Saturday. Lately, he and I have to confess, they have seldom done very well, but Bolton was my friend's first love amongst football clubs because he was born nearer to Burnden Park than to any other Football League club's ground.

He probably has not seen Bolton, the town, its football ground, for twenty years or so; has not lived there for the past forty years, but that was, *and still is*, his club—the one that really matters most even if, for him, the glory has faded from the years when the Trotters used to go along to Wembley every three years to play in the Cup Final—and each time came home with the trophy (in 1923, 1926 and 1929).

Come to think of it, I have a special reason for remembering the 1929 Final. My club, Portsmouth, had given me the very best birthday present a nine-year-old football-daft boy could wish for, just two years before, when they won promotion to the First Division (after only seven years a member of the Football League!). Then in 1929 they made their first-ever appearance in the F.A. Cup Final. Alas, that time there was no birthday present for me as Bolton

won by two goals to nil, but Pompey's great days were still to come. In what was left of the pre-Second World War period they made five-yearly trips to Wembley for the Final and were unluckily beaten by Manchester City in 1934 (*unfairly*, the old boys will still argue, as they contend that Pompey's great centre-half of the time, Jimmy Allen, was well and truly clobbered before City got their goals. Funny how, as Geoff Ellis mentions in another article in this annual, some people seem to think that tough play only came into the game with increased pay and bonuses!); then splendidly in 1939 Portsmouth turned in one of the best of Cup Final performances to beat the 'certain' favourites Wolves by four goals to one.

And after the war, of course, they gathered a team of young players, most of them without having to spend a penny on transfer fees, who won the Football League Championship two seasons in succession—and there are still only a handful of clubs who have done that!

Now, of course, Pompey, like Bolton, grub around in the Second Division and as my friend dreams of Jack and Vizard and, more recently, of Nat Lofthouse and Eddie Hopkinson, so I dream of Danny McPhail, Jack Weddle, McAlinden and Guthrie, and, most of all, of Jimmy Scoular, Jack

63

Froggatt, Len Phillips, Peter Harris and Jimmy Dickinson. . . .

There's nothing unusual or exceptional in our attachment to our first-loves. Michael Parkinson can never forget Barnsley; John Arlott retains his affection for Reading; everyone who loves football, the magical game, must have this loyalty to their own club. It's a great help, financially, to any club to be enjoying a good run of success and having the turnstiles clicking merrily at every home match—but, let's face it, a heck of a lot have come along only because the team is doing well, and the team's success makes them feel entitled to crow—and sometimes make themselves a nuisance to those who want to watch the play!

Yet, I suspect that most of us, even when our loyalty is to modest, unsuccessful, unglamorous clubs, like to enjoy some of the glory reflected from a successful club—particularly when we are young fans, say around the ten- to twelve-year-old period. So that makes us choose a second-best favourite club and I would hazard a guess that for a majority of football-lovers in this country under the age of 35 that second favourite club is Manchester United.

Other clubs over the past 25 years have had their moments, with Spurs even doing what we were beginning to think was impossible—to win Cup and League in the same season (1960–61), but no other club has been so consistently top or near the top throughout the entire period. Last season United showed signs of having to struggle more than was good for their comfort but still for more Saturdays than not the biggest attendance was at Old Trafford; and still it was often United that drew the biggest attendance of the season to other grounds when they were the visitors.

The biggest attendances in the *First* Division I should have written, because although, as ever, the First Division matches attracted the biggest crowds, something remarkable was happening in the Third Division of the Football League during the season 1970–71.

I follow the world football scene more closely than most. I am delighted with the way that the game has spread throughout the world; thrilled by the great competitions, at club and national level, that involve the players of so many different countries; appreciative of what we, in Britain, can learn from the skills and the tactics of foreign players and clubs. But when it comes down to the essential appeal of the game, the close identification of supporters with their local club, I am sure that nowhere is this so inherent as here at home.

I know the extent to which Brazil are football-mad; the fanatical support that the Italians show for their top clubs; but where else would you find the crowd support for a *Third* Division side that Aston Villa received last season? Nor, mark you, are the First and Second Divisions of our Football League made up of only fourteen or sixteen clubs each as are those of most foreign countries. No, there were forty-four clubs enjoying a higher status than the Villa as the season opened with this famous old Birmingham club going off to Chesterfield to play their very first match in the Third Division—after a Football League membership that had begun in 1888! And what happened at Chesterfield—an attendance of 16,760, which is more than *most* European First Division clubs ever get at their matches! And one week later Aston Villa played their first home match in the Third Division—against Plymouth, and few are likely to believe that it was any particular attraction from the visitors that brought almost thirty thousand (actually 29,205) to Villa Park. A bigger attendance, incidentally, than there was at any of the eleven Second Division matches played the same August afternoon; and bigger than five of the eleven First Division matches.

And with some ups and downs, usually because of the weather, the same story was repeated throughout the season—of a remarkably high level of support for the club at home marches, and, a welcome financial boost for the other clubs in the Division, bumper attendances wherever

Two great clubs of yesterday in a 1970–71 season Second Division match. Bolton's Alan Boswell punches the ball away from Blackburn's Bryan Conlon

Terry Poole of Huddersfield

Bob Wilson, Arsenal

Paddy Rice, Arsenal

Villa were the visitors.

Aston Villa won the last of their record-holding seven F.A. Cup Finals back in 1957 (and the one before that in 1920). They last won the League Championship (for the sixth time) in 1910. It was in 1897 that they followed Preston North End (1889) in winning Cup and League in the same season (Spurs, and now Arsenal, are the only other clubs to do the 'double').

It is unlikely therefore that there are many fans around who can really recall the great days of the Villa—yet their greatness, of which boys like myself could only read in the late twenties and thirties when it was already history, still lingers and their visit attracted thousands to the grounds of the other Third Division clubs.

I have already mentioned that my football-spectating effectively dates from the time when Pompey won promotion to the First Division—the season 1926–27. Readers who have learned their football history dates, even if they may be less sure of those of the various Reform Bills and Enclosure Acts, can probably conclude from that 1926 date what club became my second favourite club—Huddersfield Town.

To most youngsters today I suppose that, unless they live in the town, Huddersfield are reckoned only as a club that, after a lapse of fourteen years (but to youngsters that might as well be *forty*!), have just got back into the First Division. To football-lovers over fifty years of age Huddersfield remain one of the greatest of post-1920 clubs.

It was at the end of the 1919–20 season that Huddersfield finished second to Tottenham in the Second Division to earn entry to

George Best in action against Huddersfield

the First Division for the first time. In truth, although I did not learn this until some time after I first fell in love with Huddersfield in 1926, the club had seemed likely at one period to fold up during the season 1919–20. Very, very short of funds, there had been serious discussion about moving the club to the ground of the Leeds City club that had been expelled from the Football Association for making illegal payments during the war years. The prospect of losing their professional football club to Leeds stirred sufficient support amongst the Huddersfield townsmen (most of whom were Rugby League supporters) to save the Second Division club—and the players then proceeded to justify that support by, as I have mentioned, gaining promotion—and also by reaching the Final of the F.A. Cup where they were only beaten in extra time by Aston Villa by the only goal of the match. That goal, incidentally, like many that have had exceptional value to a team, was something of a fluke when the ball from a corner-kick

hit Villa's inside-right, Kirton, on the back of his neck and went into the goal—the 'hero' did not immediately realise that he had scored a Cup-winning goal!

By 1926, when I first peered through the railings at Fratton Park watching football, Huddersfield had done what no other club, even in the years when the First Division consisted of only eighteen or less clubs, had ever done—they won the Football League Championship *three* seasons in succession (1923–24, 1924–25, 1925–26). This was something for the fitba'-daft eight-year-old to *read* about—unlike today when, thanks to television, boys in every party of the country can *see* the great teams like Leeds, Arsenal, Manchester City and Manchester United, Tottenham and Chelsea, Liverpool and Everton, in action on the television screen.

But Pompey's promotion gave me the chance to actually *see* my Huddersfield heroes, and, in particular, the never-to-be-forgotten Alex Jackson, signed from Aberdeen in 1925, and, for me, one of the greatest

Eddie Gray of Leeds in action

Peter Storey and Terry Hennessey in a tangle with Derby's Alan Durban waiting the outcome

of all the great players I have ever seen.

During the time when Harold Wilson was Prime Minister I read a story about him that said in his wallet he still carried a small picture of the Huddersfield team of that period, and I could understand what that meant to him—a Yorkshire boy for whom, of course, Huddersfield was *the* club. I have never forgotten to check how they have got on each Saturday soon after finding out how Pompey had fared.

Huddersfield did not continue their run of Championship successes but they came pretty close—runners-up for the next two seasons. Then, as their League position dropped a bit they challenged strongly for the F.A. Cup that they had won in 1922. Now in 1928 they reached the Final—but

lost 1–3 to Blackburn Rovers; in 1929 they reached the Semi-Final (lost 1–3 to Bolton Wanderers); and in 1930 they reached the Final—and lost to Arsenal by two goals to nil.

It was a sign of things to come that Arsenal should have won the 1930 Cup Final because they were more surely the masters throughout the thirties than any other club have been in a decade. And, significantly, the man who did most to lay the foundation for their success was Herbert Chapman who had managed Huddersfield from 1922 to 1925.

Arsenal, first elected to the Second Division of the Football League in 1893, promoted to the First Division at the end of the 1903–4 season, relegated at the end

Arsenal v. Forest with John Radford closely challenged by two Forest defenders

of the 1912–13 season, but restored to the First Division by election when the number of clubs was extended from twenty to twenty-two when competitive football was resumed in 1919–20 after the First World War, had never won League or Cup when Herbert Chapman took them over. What happened next is best shown in tabulated form:

1925–26   Arsenal were runners-up to Huddersfield (Chapman's old club) in the League Championship.

1926–27   Arsenal were runners-up in the F.A. Cup competition.

1929–30   Arsenal won the F.A. Cup.

1930–31   Arsenal won the League Championship with a then record number of points—66.

1931–32   Arsenal were the runners-up in both the F.A. Cup competition and the League Championship.

1932–33   Arsenal won the League Championship.

1933–34   At the time of Herbert Chapman's death on 6 January 1934, Arsenal were at the head of the League table.

Arsenal, in fact, went on to win the Championship that season—and one season later they emulated Huddersfield's feat of the previous decade by completing a hat-trick of League Championship successes. Their manager, carrying on the work started by Chapman and utilising the fine wealth of talent developed by him (Arsenal Reserves won the London (now Football) Combination six

Charlie George, the bright young Arsenal star, in action against Crystal Palace

seasons in succession during Chapman's reign), was George Allison, and he saw Arsenal to a further Championship triumph in 1937–38 and to a F.A. Cup Final victory over Sheffield United in 1936.

Small wonder that those who first came under the spell of football during the thirties are likely to claim the Arsenal as their second favourite club—unless they are Londoners when it would be their first love!

And today? Manchester United, as I have mentioned, were the tops in the fifties and for most of the sixties, but if I were about ten years old today I think that, outside of my home town club, I would have second-best affection for Leeds United for their consistency since they won the Second Division Championship in 1964. Since then they have won League and Cup, plus the Fairs Cup—but what they deserve to win is the European Champions Cup. Maybe they soon will. . . . or will Arsenal do it first?

SCOTTISH PICTURES

*Hands up! Colin Stein shows his delight at scoring his second and Rangers' fourth goal in a 4–1 win over Dunfermline
—and the Ibrox crowd copy his gesture*

73

(Top left) *1971—and Bertie Auld still gets a run in Celtic's strip. Queen of the South's keeper, Alan Ball, stopped Bertie's attempt to score this time, however*

(Bottom left) *April 1970 and in the Scottish Cup Final Aberdeen succeed in breaking Celtic's recent monopoly of Scottish football honours. Aberdeen's scorers, Derek McKay and Joe Harper, hold the Cup*

(Right) *Sandy Jardine (Rangers) and John McLaughlin (Falkirk) in action*

(Below) *What else can a keeper do but sit and wish that he was somewhere else when, like Dundee's Ally Donaldson, he has to pick the ball out of the net for the eighth time? And to make it worse, Celtic—who else?—went on their eight goals rampage at Dundee's own Dens Park*

THE ALL STARS QUIZ
by JULIAN JEFFERY

Martin Peters effectively, but illegally, brought down playing for England against Rumania in Mexico. Who scored for England in that match?—see Question 4

Six questions on the 1970 World Cup to start with . . .

1. Brazil met Italy in the 1970 World Cup Final in Mexico City's Aztec Stadium. Both countries had won the competition twice before and the Jules Rimet trophy would become the property of the first country to win it three times. In the event Brazil beat the European Champions by 4 goals to 1. Do you know the other two years in which Brazil won the World Cup, and where were these Finals staged?

2. One other country apart from Italy has won the World Championship twice; in 1930 when the competition was started, and in 1950 when Brazil, the host nation, were the beaten finalists. Which country?

3. 1970 was not a happy year for England, the World Cup holders. They were knocked out in the quarter-finals in Mexico by West Germany, the country they had soundly beaten in the 1966 Final. Mullery and Peters gave England a 2–0 lead, but the Germans fought back through Beckenbauer and Seeler. Their winning goal, in extra time, came from the player who finished as the tournament's top scorer with ten goals. Can you name him?

4. Who scored England's first goal in Mexico in the opening match with Rumania?

5. One of Brazil's star forwards set up a new scoring record, finding the net in every match in the final stages. Which player?

6. An easy question to close this section. In which country will the 1974 World Cup Finals be held?

The oldest and the greatest competition of all . . . the F.A. Cup . . .

7. 1970 saw the F.A. Cup Final at Wembley between Chelsea and Leeds United end in a draw after extra time. The last occasion on which this happened was in 1912 when Barnsley drew 0–0 with West Bromwich Albion at the Crystal Palace. The 1970 replay took place at Old Trafford, Manchester. With the score deadlocked at 1–1 after 90 minutes, the match again went into extra time. What was the final score?

8. The first F.A. Cup competition in 1871–72 attracted only fifteen entries. The Wanderers beat the Royal Engineers 1–0 in the Final at Kennington Oval. In which season was the first Final ever held at the Wembley Stadium?

9. Leicester City must be the unluckiest team in the F.A. Cup in recent years. They have appeared in three Wembley Finals since 1960 and have been beaten in all three. On a happier note; which team has won the Cup the most times since 1960?

Action at Old Trafford in the 1970 replayed F.A. Cup Final—does it help you with Question 7?

Into Europe . . .

10. Although 1970 was a disappointing year for England's international team, it was a great year for British clubs in the major European competitions. Manchester City brought the Cup-winners Cup to England for the third time, beating Gornik Zabrze of Poland by 2 goals to 1 at the Prater Stadium in Vienna. Who are the two other English clubs who have won the Cup-winners Cup?

11. Arsenal made it a hat-trick of English wins in the Fairs Cup. In 1968 Leeds beat Ferencvaros of Hungary 1–0 in the two-leg Final, and a year later the Fairs Cup went to Newcastle, who thrashed Ujpest Dozsa, another Hungarian team, 6–2 on aggregate. In the 1970 Final Arsenal found themselves 3–1 down after the first leg in Belgium, but goals from Kelly, Radford and Sammels saw them win 3–0 at Highbury. Who were their opponents in the Final?

12. Glasgow Celtic were a disappointment in the European Champions Cup Final, going down 2–1 to Feyenoord of Rotterdam after extra time. Celtic showed none of the fire, skill and confidence which had seen them beat Leeds United in both legs of their Semi-Final, and Feyenoord deservedly took the Cup to the Netherlands for the first time. Where was this Final played?

Up for the Cup . . .

Apart from the F.A. and European Cups, there are many other knock-out competitions to excite and interest the football fan. Here are some questions on these other 'cup' competitions.

13. The F.A. Amateur Cup was started in 1893–94, the Old Carthusians beating the Casuals 2–1 in the first Final. The 1970 Final was an all-London affair, Enfield thrashing Dagenham 5–1, but the team which has won the Amateur Cup the most times comes from the north of England. Can you name the team?

14. In season 1969–70 a new knock-out competition for non-league clubs was held. The Final of this competition, the F.A. Challenge Trophy, was staged at Wembley Stadium. Which two teams took part in this Final, and what was the score?

15. The Welsh Cup competition is dominated by the Welsh clubs that play in the Football League. The winners of the Welsh Cup qualify for the European Cup-winners Cup, and the competition has therefore provided Cardiff City with a passport to Europe. In the ten seasons from 1960 to 1970 Cardiff won the Welsh Cup no fewer than six times. The Final of 1963 was the last occasion on which a club from outside the Football League won the Welsh Cup, beating Newport County 2–1. Which club?

16. In the first-ever Final of the Football League Cup Aston Villa beat Rotherham United 3–2 on aggregate. In which season was this?

17. In season 1966–67 the two-leg system was dropped for the Final of League Cup, and the game was held at Wembley. Queens Park Rangers, then in the Third Division, shocked the football world by beating First Division West Bromwich Albion 3–2. Two years later another Third Division club won the League Cup Final at Wembley, beating Arsenal 3–1. Can you name the club?

18. The 1970–71 League Cup also saw some giant-killing. One Second and one Third Division club reached the semi-finals. Bristol City went out to Spurs, but Aston Villa drew at Old Trafford and then beat Manchester United 2–1 in the second leg, despite a fine individualist goal which put United ahead. Who scored this goal?

19. While we are on the question of goal scorers, who got Chelsea's winning goal in the sensational 1970 F.A. Cup Final replay at Old Trafford?

20. Now a question for supporters of Irish teams. Linfield hold the best record in the Irish Cup in recent years. They appeared in seven of the ten Finals from 1960 to 1970. How many did they win?

What do you know about Scottish football . . .

21. Scottish Cup Finals are played at Hampden Park, Glasgow. Which Scottish league club owns this famous ground?

Martin Chivers, being hugged by Martin Peters, scores in Spurs F.L. Cup semi-final against Bristol City—see Question 18

22. Can you name the grounds of Hibernian, Hearts and Rangers?

23. Celtic and Rangers, the top Glasgow clubs, have dominated Scottish football for the last decade. In the ten seasons from 1960 to 1970 these two great clubs between them won the Scottish League Championship eight times, the League Cup nine times, and the Scottish Cup seven times. Only once in these ten years did neither team reach the Scottish Cup Final. That was in 1968 when Dunfermline met Hearts at Hampden Park. What was the result of this game?

24. In 1970 Scotland, England and Wales shared the Home International Championship. When was Scotland last the sole winners of the competition?

25. Apart from Celtic's two appearances in the European Cup Final, only one other Scottish club has reached the Final of a major European competition. Rangers lost 4–1 on aggregate to Fiorentina in the first-ever Final of the Cup-winners Cup in 1961, and then in the 1967 Final of the same competition they were beaten 1–0 in Nuremburg. Who were their opponents?

Five simple questions to finish with . . .

26. Who won the Watney Cup, the first sponsored football competition in Britain, at the beginning of the 1970–71 season?

27. Which well-known English First Division teams are known by the following nicknames . . . the Saints, the Gunners, the Pensioners?

28. Which home clubs play at Anfield, Craven Cottage and Fratton Park?

29. When Bradford Park Avenue failed to gain re-election to the Football League in 1970 which club took their place, and in what league had this club been playing?

30. How long is the duration of play in a Football League game?

Answers on page 105

79

Jack Charlton and Alan Birchenall looking a bit cold—there's snow on their boots!

WITH PALACE in the BIG TIME

ALAN BIRCHENALL

What delight! Alan Birchenall after scoring for Palace against his old club, Chelsea

EVERYONE WAS DETERMINED THAT PALACE SHOULD NOT REMAIN JUST ANOTHER FIRST DIVISION CLUB AND I AM CONVINCED THAT THIS REALLY GO-AHEAD ATTITUDE PERSUADED ME TO SIGN

MOVING from one club to another can so often be an extremely dicey business even in the case of the most experienced and hardened professional.

When I signed for Chelsea from Sheffield United in 1967, I was convinced that I would be a regular member of the Stamford Bridge outfit for some years to come. And it certainly looked that way when during

81

Alan Birchenall scoring the only goal of the match on his debut for Chelsea against Sunderland at Roker Park, December 1967

my first team début at Roker Park, Sunderland, I not only fitted in well with the rest of the lads, but also scored our only goal.

But after a couple of very successful campaigns with Chelsea, Lady Luck began to dominate my career in no uncertain manner.

In retrospect I was in many ways given a raw deal. Not, I hasten to add, by Chelsea, but literally by fate itself.

I began the 1969–70 season with a tremendous bang, and played what was probably my finest game for the 'Blues' in our convincing First Division home win over Arsenal. I continued the good work with two more goals in our two Football League Cup-ties with Leeds United.

My next game, which on paper looked to be a cakewalk, was against West Bromwich Albion, and during this match I received what I thought to be only a slight knee injury.

However, this knee trouble proved to be much more serious than most people thought. It wasn't really that bad as football injuries go; in fact, sometimes I did not even

notice it. But all the same it was there right enough, niggling me whenever I attempted to kick a ball.

Meanwhile, during the time I was out of the side guys such as Ian Hutchinson and teenager Alan Hudson were establishing themselves in the first team, adding that something extra to the Chelsea line-up as well.

So when I was eventually declared fully fit, I had to be content with reserve team football, which I can assure you can depress even the most phlegmatic guy. Playing before less than 1,000 fans at Stamford Bridge is certainly not the ideal way to boost one's waning confidence.

Then at last, after many weeks of waiting, my chance came to show exactly what I could do for the first team. Peter Osgood was chosen at the eleventh hour to represent England in Belgium, so I was drafted into the attack as one of the main strikers for our home fixture with Newcastle United.

Everything was going well for me, and I was just about to slot the ball past the

'Magpies' 'keeper Iam McFaul when we collided, and I was rushed to hospital with a nasty cut in my knee.

The cut was so deep and wide that it even led to ominous doubts about my future in professional soccer. But I overcame all this adversity, and was declared fit several weeks before even the most optimistic expert had anticipated. In fact, I was fit enough to play a couple of league games prior to that F.A. Cup Final epic with Leeds United.

But those end-of season games did not fool me one little bit. I knew only too well that it would need a miracle for me to win my place back on a regular basis. Okay, I would still remain a member of manager Dave Sexton's first team squad, but as far as I was concerned this simply wasn't my scene at all.

I have been playing First Division football for some eight years or so, therefore I obviously had to leave Chelsea, although I had always been happy there and made many friends among my team-mates.

Dave Sexton had bought me for £100,000 from Sheffield United. So he was determined not to lose any bread on the deal.

Several clubs approached Chelsea, and at one time I was in a considerable dilemma about where I should move to. When Crystal Palace approached me, I really did not know what to think during my journey to Selhurst Park to discuss terms.

After my initial visit to Palace I was struck

A 1970 London 'derby'—Chelsea v. Spurs with John Hollins, Alan Birchenall and Martin Peters in action

October sunshine at Selhurst Park as Alan Birchenall gets round Albion's John Talbut but Jimmy Cumbes has safely gathered the ball

almost immediately by the progressive attitude which exists at the club. Everyone was determined that Palace should not remain just another First Division club, and I am convinced that this really go-ahead attitude persuaded me to sign on the dotted line.

Since my first match for Crystal Palace, I have in my opinion been playing better than at any stage in my career.

Now, of course, we are well and truly in the big time, and our main aim must be European competition and all the incentives playing in Europe can bring. If this happens then the football-mad fans of London, S.E.25, can for the first time look forward to being emotionally involved in the glamorous world of a major European knock-out tournament.

84

A MAN WITH A PRICE ON HIS HEAD
Henry Newton

Henry Newton in action on his Everton debut

WHEN I AWOKE THE NEXT MORN-
ING, IT SUDDENLY HIT ME THAT A
TREMENDOUS LOT WOULD BE EX-
PECTED OF A £150,000 PLAYER

NOW I know what it's like to be a man
with a price on your head—a professional footballer rated at £150,000 in the
transfer market . . . and being assessed as
such, by the critics and the public.

It's just about a year since I joined
Everton; had I not left Nottingham Forest
when I did, I believe I would have stayed

John Hurst (Everton) and John Pratt (Spurs) in action

with my home-town club to the end of my career. My transfer to Everton was make or break.

I was ambitious, I wanted to join the best team in the land; I felt that I could measure up to the demands such ambition would require. After I had made my League debut for Everton at Highbury—and we had been given a four-goal hiding—I knew for certain that the going was going to be hard.

Many a time, in the past months, I have reflected upon a resolution I made within 24 hours of having signed for Everton.

I wrote my signature on the dotted line, on a Tuesday afternoon last October. When I awoke the next morning, it suddenly hit me that a tremendous lot would be expected of a £150,000 player.

There and then, I resolved that I was going to try to ignore the price tag—I couldn't forget it, but I was determined that it wasn't going to change my whole style of play.

I realised that the critics—and the fans on the terraces—would be weighing me up, over the next few weeks. And after that Highbury debacle, I determined that I wasn't going to let THAT linger in my mind, either.

I kept telling myself that I hadn't fixed the fee, that I had been signed to become a member of a TEAM. And that it was as a team player, not an individualist, that Everton wanted to employ me.

One of the things I had to face, of course, was the fact that—£150,000 or not—there were so many talented players at Goodison Park that no player could ever be sure of his place.

Indeed, after one game, I had to resign myself to sitting and sweating it out, for Everton were involved in a European Cup-tie against the West German club, Moenchengladbach—and I was not eligible to play.

Naturally, Everton reverted to their old formation, and I found myself on the sidelines for a league game or two, as well.

No player likes to be out of action, but I recognised that even a £150,000 player had to accept this concept of modern-day soccer. Team demands are over-riding considerations.

I found myself playing at left-back later in the season. Against Liverpool, in the derby game at Anfield, I began at left-back and switched to midfield when Howard Kendall went off injured, and Keith Newton came on to take over the No. 3 spot.

Later still, Keith Newton—an England World Cup man in Mexico remember—was in the reserves, while I occupied his old left-back position in the first team.

In the reserves, too, were goalkeeper Gordon West—another player capped by England—and Jimmy Husband, an England

Under-23 man.

And Brian Labone, who had also played for England in Mexico, found himself in and out of the first team last season, as well.

I think the knowledge that other talented players were having to soldier on in the reserves was a help to me. A help in the sense that the glare of publicity faded somewhat, and I was able to get on with the job of settling down to find my feet and my form.

Instead of being frightened that I might find myself in the reserves, I was able to melt into the overall pattern, so to speak, because there were so many players of great reputation finding that times had changed for them.

On the other hand, of course, the knowledge that these players were itching to regain their first-team spots acted as a spur to us all—collectively.

In goal, at full-back, in the middle line and up front, there were few who could rely upon their place, week in, week out. So I became one of many . . . just another player getting on with the job of doing his best—and going that little bit harder, because of the challenge from players on the sidelines.

I even found that I hadn't much time to play golf—and with a handicap of eight, I was a pretty keen golfer. But making the grade at Everton was my top priority.

Many a time in the past months I have thought back to certain games—the time Fred Pickering made his debut for Everton, against Nottingham Forest; the game I played for Forest against Wolves; and an F.A. Cup-tie involving Forest and Everton.

The day 'Pick' made his bow for the Blues, I was in the Forest team. We scored a goal that day at Goodison—but Everton rattled in six. And Pickering finished with a hat-trick!

In the Cup against Everton—it was a sixth-round tie—Jimmy Husband put two past Forest. But winger Ian Storey-Moore snatched a hat-trick to put Everton out and Forest into the Semi-Finals.

And when Forest played Wolves at

Frank Lampard about to tackle Alan Ball

Molineux they were trailing by three goals at half-time. In the second half, I moved upfield, and we finished up by making it a 3–3 draw. And I scored twice!

So, on occasions when I've pondered on the perils of being a £150,000 signing, on the battle to get into and maintain a first-team place with Everton, I've also remembered games like those I've just mentioned.

Games which show that football can make you a winner, when you think you're going to be a loser.

In Nottingham, they used to call my right foot 'Enery's 'Ammer, the way I could blast the ball for goal. I scored quite a few goals in my Forest career. Now I've settled down at Goodison, the price on my head doesn't seem to matter any more . . . and I'm hoping this season 'Enery's 'Ammer will collect a few goals for Everton, too.

A JOB WITH KICKS
by GEOFF ELLIS

Trouble at Parkhead in an old firm, Celtic-Rangers, match but 'Tiny' Wharton the referee is well equipped to deal with such situations

VIOLENCE ON THE FOOTBALL FIELDS ALL OVER BRITAIN WAS ALMOST A WEEKLY COMPLAINT DURING THE 1970–71 SEASON

VIOLENCE on the football fields all over Britain was almost a weekly complaint during the 1970–71 season. Even amateur players did not escape criticism. There was a suggestion even that clubs and managers should be fined when players were 'booked' by the referees.

One player spoke out. Newcastle United's Welsh international centre-forward was quoted as saying that he had taken a fearful

Crystal Palace keeper John Jackson being strongly challenged for the ball by Stoke centre-half Dennis Smith

amount of injuries over the years and that violence had increased to such an extent that he 'had gone chicken'. His displays of courage on the field, however, belied the fact that he was afraid. But violence on the increase? To find out if it was so a poll was taken of five forwards, whose job is to score goals, and five defenders. You have to make up your mind after reading their views:

Geoff Hurst (West Ham and England): 'The game is getting more violent. I suppose you can track down the root cause to the financial rewards. You've got to accept that when you go into the penalty area you are going to get kicked and the best you can hope for is some protection from the referee. At the same time you have to accept that it is now part of the game. I make a count of the knocks and bruises after every game. They are always there.'

Ron Davies (Southampton and Wales): 'It is quite violent these days, more than it used to be. But it is not difficult to under-stand why defenders are trying to intimidate forwards. If I score I could cost the oppos-ing centre-half a £50 winning bonus, and he's not going to love me for that, is he?'

Alun Evans (Liverpool and England Under-23): 'There's a lot more stick than when I first started. Mind you, it depends on who you are playing against whether they play you or the ball. There are teams who play fair and hard and those who play hard and unfair.'

Mick Jones (Leeds United and England): 'Yes, it's got tougher, with so much at stake these days. Bonuses and European competi-tions make it necessary for players to give all or nothing. But it's no use showing fear. If a player starts kicking you it is best to consider it as a backhanded compliment. The defender is there to stop you and he WILL stop you. That's the way the game is going.'

No—Saints' keeper Eric Martin is not bawling at Peter Osgood after some violent clash. It was his own back—who has slipped away!—who incurred Martin's wrath when he passed the ball back with Peter Osgood almost able to intercept

Mike England and Brian Kidd challenging for the ball

Brian Kidd (Manchester United and England): 'It seems harder to get goals now than when I first came into the team. Defences are more organised and you are bound to take some stick. But you've got to be prepared to take this punishment.'

Now for the defence! Five defenders hit back, verbally, of course!

Mike England (Spurs and Wales): 'It's nonsense to suggest that forwards are getting kicked so often. Defences are so well organised now that I imagine forwards are suffering from frustration because they are finding goals harder to come by. That often means that it is the defenders that start getting kicked.'

Violence on the football field—but it's a white-shirted spectator who has floored Jim Fraser in a Rangers-Dunfermline match at Ibrox

Tony Book (Manchester City): 'There definitely has been no increase in tough play, but there has been an increase in the number of forwards who shout about it. And remember, the attackers can do a bit of kicking themselves.'

Ron Harris (Chelsea): 'I can understand how forwards feel because they are trying to do their jobs, which is scoring goals. But I don't see what they are cribbing about . . . playing football and getting the odd kick now and again is a lot better than working in a factory and getting a finger caught in a lathe.'

David Sadler (Manchester United and England): 'I have played up front as well as at the back and in those days I didn't think the tackling was excessively unfair. I think that still applies. It is a physical game with a lot of body contact which means that somebody is going to get hurt. Defenders get their share. There is nothing worse than an elbow in the eye.' (Sadler sustained a broken cheekbone in December 1970.)

Tommy Smith (Liverpool): 'It is a highly competitive game and that means everyone is keyed up, but we rarely see anyone deliberately kick. When it does happen there is a 50–50 chance that it is a forward kicking a defender out of frustration.'

Alun Evans and Bobby Moore in a duel

The North HAVE dominated
SAYS STAN LIVERSEDGE

The back-alleys of industrial towns were the first pitches of many a great player but it is not often that a great player lends a hand in a back-alley kickabout as did the former Benfica and Portugal keeper Costa Pereira with these lads of Brunswick Street, Garston, Liverpool

IS THERE ANY SUBSTANCE IN THE CLAIM THAT THE NORTH BREEDS HARDIER PLAYERS, MORE PROFESSIONAL PLAYERS, BETTER ALL-ROUND TEAMS?

A FEW thousand words have already been written about whether clubs in the north are harder than clubs in the south (to put it mildly!). And whatever your opinion, the fact cannot be denied that northern sides HAVE dominated these past few seasons.

Take Europe, for example: Manchester

Tommy Smith and Steve Perryman

United (and Glasgow Celtic) won the European Cup. In the Cup-winners Cup, Tottenham and West Ham scored the British successes in 1963 and 1965, respectively—but then it was the turn of Manchester City to lift the trophy.

As for the Fairs Cup, the list reads like this: Arsenal, Newcastle United, Leeds United. One team from the south, two from the north.

And what about the First Division championship?—Leeds, Everton, Manchester City, Manchester United, Liverpool, Burnley . . . and Ipswich and Tottenham. In

Howard Kendall and Ray Kennedy

ten years only two southern clubs became champions.

In the F.A. Cup the honours have been more even, over the past ten years—Tottenham (three times), West Ham, Chelsea, West Bromwich Albion, Manchester United, Liverpool, Everton, Manchester City—these have been the winners.

Last season, we saw the emergence of Arsenal, Spurs and Chelsea as title hopes from the south, while Leeds United dominated the northern challengers.

IS there any substance in the claim that the north breeds hardier players, more

Eyes on the ball—Alan Ball and Peter Storey

professional players, better all-round teams? Alan Ball, manager of Preston North End, is one who thinks there is . . . although, of course, he's a northerner!

But Ball believes that the environment plays some part in the make-up of players and teams. 'Our northern towns and cities are grimier, maybe grimmer, than those in the south,' he says.

'And our footballers in this part of the world reflect this in this approach to the game. They play it harder . . . yet they're as skilled as any you can name.'

In case anyone wants to raise a dissentient voice here, it is only fair to go through the players Sir Alf Ramsey has chosen for England, in recent years—and the north dominates, once more.

Gordon Banks, Peter Shilton—one from Sheffield, the other from Leicester. Tommy Wright, Keith Newton, Emlyn Hughes—Liverpool, Manchester, Barrow. Norman Hunter, Nobby Stiles, Jackie Charlton, Brian Labone—all northerners again.

And up front, you have men like Alan Ball, Colin Bell, Francis Lee, Brian Kidd, Allan Clarke, Bobby Charlton, Geoff Hurst.

When you take away these names, what have you left? From the south . . . Bobby Moore, Martin Peters and Alan Mullery.

Last season, Arsenal, Tottenham and Chelsea were chasing Leeds for the title. Go through the personnel of these London clubs—and you find names from the north, or from Scotland and Ireland.

Arsenal: Bob Wilson (Chesterfield), Bob McNab (Huddersfield), Eddie Kelly and Frank McLintock (Glasgow), George Armstrong (Hepburn), Ray Kennedy (Whitley Bay), George Graham (Lanarkshire).

Tottenham: Pat Jennings and Joe Kinnear (Ireland), Cyril Knowles (Fitzwilliam) and Mike England (North Wales)—who both played for northern clubs.

Chelsea: Eddie McCreadie (Glasgow), Paddy Mulligan (Dublin), Tommy Baldwin (Gateshead), Ian Hutchinson (Derby), Charlie Cooke (Scotland).

If you go back to the foundation of the Football League, you can see where the game has its roots. These were the dozen founder-members: Accrington, Aston Villa, Blackburn Rovers, Bolton Wanderers, Burnley, Derby County, Everton, Notts County, Preston North End, Stoke City, West Bromwich Albion, Wolverhampton Wanderers.

Lancashire and the Black Country pioneered the way—areas of England where there has long been grime, muck—and money which has had to be hard-earned.

The more salubrious south has not had to fight quite so hard, maybe, for survival. The lads down the pit found an escape route in soccer. 'Shout down a coal mine,' they used to say of the north-east, 'and up will come a footballer.'

This season, clearly, the pressure from the south will be greater than ever before. The 60s saw the northern clubs dominate, after that early double by the Spurs. Now Arsenal have emulated the Spurs.

Perhaps the portents were there, when Chelsea lifted the F.A. Cup from Leeds United, in that marathon battle two seasons ago. Although Chelsea, even then, had their slice of luck in coming up against a side running out of steam, from the effort of trying to achieve a magical treble.

Perhaps, above all, the supporters of the northern clubs have played their part—they have been more partisan, more keenly involved and identified with their respective clubs.

Today, perhaps, the wheel is about to turn full circle, and bring us a spell when Arsenal, Tottenham and Chelsea will be the teams of whom we must beware.

But even now, when you consider Liverpool, Leeds, Everton and the Manchester clubs, it is probably fair to say that if the era of northern dominance is ending, the balance of power is shifting only to a more equal position.

For, unless there is a sudden inexplicable somersault in form, it will still be a while before the southern fans can claim, in truth: 'OUR teams ARE the greatest.'

Sponsored football in England—Sir Stanley Rous and Dave Mackay holding the Watney Cup first won by Derby County in August 1970

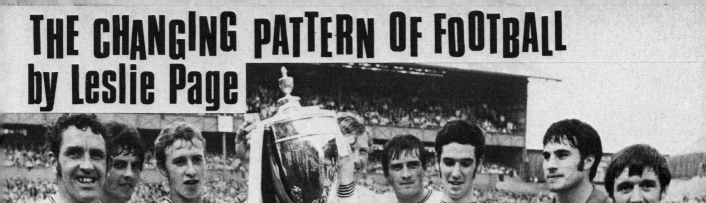

THE CHANGING PATTERN OF FOOTBALL
by Leslie Page

Some of the happy Derby players—with Cup and personal tankards—after they beat Manchester United to win the Watney Cup

IF WE CAN CREATE A COMPETITION, SUCH AS THE TEXACO CUP ... IT FOLLOWS THAT ADDITIONAL SPONSORSHIP MUST BE ON ITS WAY

WITHIN a decade British soccer underwent a very considerable change. It is not the purpose here to decide whether the change was for better or worse. It happened —now we must live with it.

But, after change has affected evolution, it must, of necessity, be followed by even

April 1970: Joe Mercer and Tony Book show off the European Cup Winners Cup to the citizens of Manchester

more radical change. In seeking to look into the future, guesswork and anticipation play a considerable role. The ideas of one correspondent will not align with those of others. Prognostication can always be called the substitute for the crystal ball. One may be no better than the other.

A little over ten years ago, two major factors stood out as landmarks for the future. The position of the professional soccer player in modern society and the advance in playing techniques outside these islands.

It was obvious that the so-called 'mini-mum wage' had to be brought to an end. The soccerman was bent on achieving his rightful place and extracting his due rewards. This he has done and for many this factor alone has altered soccer beyond all recall.

Within a vast sporting industry, higher wages, bonuses and other financial payments have forced costs to rise at an alarming rate which would have brought problems enough. Added to this, as with all other industrial enterprises, there is the spectre of deflation bringing in its wake the constant necessity to inject more and more money

May 1970: Frank McLintock and the Mayor of Islington show off the Fairs Cup to the citizens of North London

into clubs which do not find competitive success.

In four divisions of the Football League, there can only be a limited number of top clubs. The honours go round and round, but some find they do not go round enough. Outside the four divisions remain clubs which feel, strongly, they could provide more entertainment and better opportunities for success.

The time is almost upon us, I feel, when the Football League will start to make a forward move to create a much larger League combination which would, once and for all, end the criticism of 'closed shop' and provide equal chances for nearly all.

The senior division, whether it is styled 'Premier' or 'First', is likely to become smaller since the senior clubs are now engaged upon so many fronts that domestic league encounters need to be restricted lest the strictly academic battle for points, as it so often becomes, reduces a club's strength to the point where it becomes farcical.

The status of senior clubs must change season by season and they will be forced to throw aside their fears of dropping to levels they could not previously contemplate. The world of sport is an industry in the modern sense and it must be run on strictly practical lines lest chaos intervene.

We will assume, for example, that the Football League—whether in that guise or some other—is expanded to six divisions, it follows, in my estimation, that in addition to league competition and the already established Football League Cup, there will be other honours at which clubs can aim.

If we can create a competition, such as the Texaco Cup, within British soccer for those leading contenders to Europe who do not actually go into Europe in a particular season, it follows that additional sponsorship must be on its way.

The Football League already sells its fixtures to the Pools Promoters and that money is most valuable to the administration. Could it be that, eventually, the League will need to look for a sponsor for the entire competition? There are many, in fact, who think that the F.A. Cup is ripe for sponsorship and if the price was right, who is to say that the Football Association could afford to refuse such an offer?

Having thrown the gauntlet of commercial sponsorship into the arena by starting at the top, it seems to me that finance of this kind will more and more find its way into soccer born of need and, as the years roll by, utter necessity.

More Cup, more League competitions flower year by year and I see no end to them. Success is the watchword for the crowds on the terraces. Success is the desire of the clubs to keep them solvent. The greater the number of competitions, the greater the number of winners.

To talk of cheapening sporting success is to ignore mental and physical need.

All these changes must be accompanied by a tightening of the reins to check permissive irresponsibility. Having accepted the club's coin, I expect to see clubs join together in an attempt to restrain players more and more in their demands for money and status.

Whether they accept the point at the moment or not, few would doubt the sense of contracting a player to one club for a full season. There would need to be provision for player signings in the case of disastrous injuries on a large scale and, possibly, other minor adjustments. But, the basic contractual arrangement makes sense.

The outsider's delight in planning the lives of others and forecasting a new policy for an industry comes as a result of our personal involvement with football. Because the world alters day by day, so must soccer if it is to continue as a part of our lives.

Money, then, has to be brought into the game in vast amounts if it is to continue on the scale of advancement upon which it has already embarked.

If we laughed at 'Super Leagues' and a foot on the Continent saying that such things would not come to pass, the truth shows it differently. The gap between the top clubs and the lower orders grows larger with every game that is played. Three European competitions already exist in which British clubs have climbed to success with tenacious application. Surely more such competitions will follow; some for the big-timers and some for the lower orders.

With so much at stake in modern soccer, the day of the full-time professional referee must arrive. At first, there might be only ten or so full-timers. I would expect to see their numbers grow. It becomes more nonsensical, season by season, that men earning modest sums, control soccermen capable of pocketing up to £200 or more a game.

Whilst I have lived with the controversy of the paid 'amateur' ever since I was a small boy, I confidently expect that good sense and economic necessity will, eventually, produce the football 'player'. It will be the end of a considerable strain when all the parties concerned come to terms with a frustrating and sterile situation.

My forecasts could be wildly 'off-centre', my hopes thrown down, but I'll be vastly surprised if the majority of my points are not accepted as valid evolutionary progression within the next ten years.

ANSWERS TO QUIZ ON P. 76

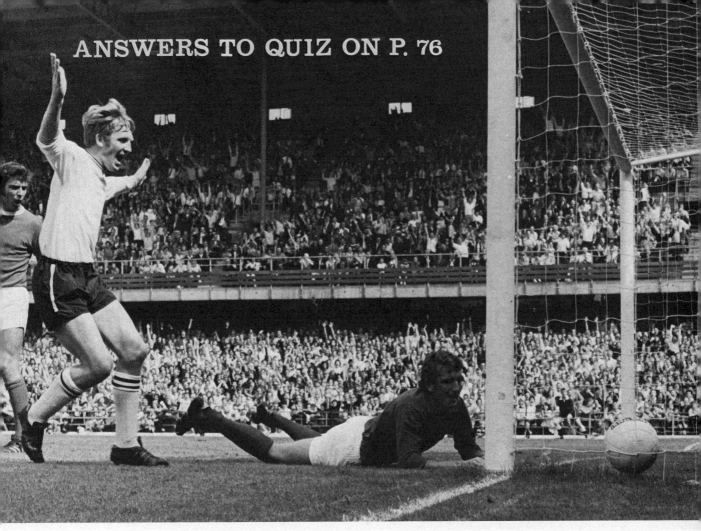

A goal for Derby against Manchester United in the 1970 Watney Cup final

1. 1958 in Sweden, and 1962 in Chile.
2. Uruguay.
3. Muller.
4. Geoff Hurst.
5. Jairzinho.
6. West Germany.
7. Chelsea 2 Leeds United 1.
8. In 1923 when Bolton Wanderers beat West Ham United 2–0.
9. Tottenham Hotspur, in 1961, 1962 and 1967.
10. Spurs in 1963, and West Ham in 1965.
11. Anderlecht.
12. San Siro Stadium, Milan.
13. Bishop Auckland, ten times.
14. Macclesfield Town 2 Telford United 0.
15. Borough United.
16. 1960–61.
17. Swindon Town.
18. Brian Kidd.
19. David Webb.
20. Four; 1960 Linfield 5 Ards 1, 1962 Linfield 4 Portadown 0, 1963 Linfield 2 Distillery 1, 1970 Linfield 2 Ballymena United 1.
21. Queens Park, the only amateur club in the Scottish League.
22. Easter Road Park, Tynecastle Park, Ibrox Stadium.
23. Dunfermline Athletic 3 Hearts 1.
24. 1967.
25. Bayern Munich.
26. Derby County.
27. Southampton, Arsenal, Chelsea.
28. Liverpool, Fulham, Portsmouth.
29. Cambridge United played in the Premier Division of the Southern League.
30. 90 minutes.